DUALITIES

Dualities

Insight On Getting Your Sh*t Together

WILL BLACK

The Balanced Self

Copyright © The Balanced Self
All rights reserved.
ISBN: 9781736089910

Contents

1	Introduction	2
2	Who Do You Want To Be?	6
3	Goal Setting	11
4	Poor Goals	21
5	Tidy Your Space	27
6	Feeling Ready	35
7	Ask For Help	40
8	Focus On What You Can Control	46
9	Worrying About Future, Regretting the Past, Staying Present	52

10	Self-Sabotage	59
11	Exercise	65
12	Surfing	69
13	Plateaus	74
14	Failure	78
15	Success	90
16	Mindset	100
17	Comparison	130
18	Removing Poisons	133
19	Procrastination	144
20	Meditation	152
21	Balance	161
22	Balance	166

For Philip and Hunter.
May you find your way.

Chapter 1

Introduction

Why Dualities? Self-help is a genre certainly not lacking in the content department. There are hundreds of authors, thousands of books published on the subject of self-improvement. From entrepreneurs, life-style gurus, business tycoons, navy SEALs, fitness experts, there is an endless stream of different perspectives on how to improve your life.

With so many options to choose from you have to ask why choose this book over any of the others that are available? With *Dualities*, my intention is to offer something unique in this world. For one, I intentionally chose to write on subjects that I am intimately connected to.

From writing and achieving goals, overcoming addiction, to creating new lasting habits like meditation, I cover many subjects that I know inside and out. When I began my journey, I looked many places for insight and guidance. It took years and without a structured roadmap took much longer than it needed to. I am forever grateful for my journey, but hopefully with *Dualities* I can save you some time and heartache. Here I aim to provide you a more concise and focused resource as to how to make meaningful and intentional life.

My own journey of growth and development was fraught with numerous challenges and obstacles that took years to overcome. From my earliest childhood memories, I was plagued mental illnesses like depression and anxiety. These conditions seeped into every aspect of my life with issues of poor self-esteem, a hopeless mindset and eventually spiraled into several forms of addiction.

Over the course of many years I was able to dig myself out of the abyss of those afflictions. Threw my own intensive research of books, podcasts, mentors, and journeys of self-discovery, I broke free of those chains. Though learning never ends and I will continue to grow, as we all do, I now feel I have mastered enough disciplines to share some insight with you.

What you now hold in your hands is the culmination of my own journey. The namesake of this book holds two parts. *Dualities* and *Insight on Getting Your Sh*t To-*

gether. The second half is named directly after a goal I started simply named, "Project Get Your Shit Together." The other half, Dualities, to me encompasses the very nature of our world. My entire ethos distilled to one word would be Balance. Finding balance in life is no simple task and has no easy solution. Hopefully I am able to bring you some clarity and insight as to how you might create that for yourself.

This book will not solve all of your problems. I cannot tell you your purpose for being here, the meaning of life, or how you will find fulfillment. It'd be nice after reading 100 or so pages that were the case and many books will promise you that, but they are lying. There is no quick fix, no easy solution.

Rather what you have here will give you the foundations to discover the solutions to those questions for yourself. I will give you step-by-step instruction on how to regain control of your life and decide for yourself what it is you want out of this experience called life.

We face many crossroads in our lives. Every day we get up and decide what person we want to be. Some days we chose to do things exactly how we've done them before. Day in, day out, we get exactly the same each time. Other days we wake up and decide we've had enough. We raise the bar for ourselves, our lives and inspire others to do the same.

Choosing to be more, do more, to grow and evolve is necessary not only for our own journey, but for all those who we surround ourselves with. We do not exist in a vacuum. Our choices impact everyone else. By raising your own standards, living a life you are truly proud of, you will inspire others to reach their highest potential. Together we can break free of our limiting beliefs and behaviors. We can chose to live in a world of our own creation.

Chapter 2

Who Do You Want To Be?

Throughout our lives we find ourselves stuck in the paradigm asking who we are. We want to find ourselves. We go out into the world, explore different jobs, meet new people. We find passions that resonate with us and others that turn us off. There is tremendous value exploring and being curious. Especially for those that feel utterly clueless as to their purpose or mission, try as much as you can. While there is certainly an enormous benefit of finding yourself through these modalities, a greater question not discussed as much is to ask *who do you want to be?*

What mark do you want to leave on the world? How do you want to be known? How do you want to be remembered? When people describe you, what sort of person do they describe? Are you kind, adventurous, cautious, caring, compassionate, wild, funny, serious, thoughtful? Are you a yogi or a mountain climber, a businessman or a firefighter, a nurse or a lawyer? There are countless ways of being, what role resonates with you?

Most people are stuck in the mold of trying to live up to other's expectations and ideas. Parents often pressure their children into careers or lifestyles they don't want. If not our parents our cultures certainly pressure us into thinking some lifestyles are superior or more worthy than others.

The wonderful news is that there is no correct answer to how you should live your life. Some people are made to burn the midnight oil, to put all their time and energy into their careers and find their fulfillment through that. Others see their jobs as a mean to cover their living expenses and find fulfillment in their hobbies, in their friends, in their community. Some are rolling stones that skip across this planet never settling, never being content in one spot, and have a thirst for exploration that can never be quenched. Others prefer the quiet life where they were born where their roots are firmly established. Most are somewhere in between. What you will find amongst the multitude of options is a series of trade-offs. Pros and cons, but no right or wrong answer.

"There is only one success, to be able to spend your life in your own way."
– Christopher Morley

Be intentional and write out what sort of person you want to be. Write down the qualities you would like to have, the hobbies you would like to do, the reputation you would be proud of. Look at it, read it over, and then truly imagine yourself as that person. Think of how it would feel. How a day in the life of the person you would like to be would feel. Imagine that day as if you have already achieved it and are experiencing it right now.

"Intentional living is the art of making our own choices before others' choices make us."
– Richie Norton

As you work on your goals and you visualize yourself as this person, slowly you will shift and this will become your reality.

Why

As you are contemplating the person you would like to be another element that will cement your vision is your reason for being, your why. Why do you want to be wealthy? Why do you want to be fit? Why do you want to travel? At the core of your desires lies the deepest truth. Keep digging until you uncover your why.

Discovering your reason for being will give you a sense of agency. Rather than blinding walking aimlessly in life, when you find your why, you will be able to move with clarity and focus. We get out of life what we put in. If you act without intention, you get aimless reward. Uncovering your truth requires introspection on your end. No one can tell you your reason for being here, it's something you have to discover for yourself. Take time and careful consideration when doing this work. Know that it won't all come at once and your reason will change as you do.

Knowing your greatest longing will anchor you and strengthen your resolve. It will allow you to persevere through the most difficult obstacles. From rejection, to cravings, fear and all the other barriers that seek to stop you, your why will guide on the correct path.

When you know your why you will be unshakable.

"The best way to predict the future is to create it."
– Unknown

Challenge: Sit down, write and think on the question of who do you want to be? Be as detailed as you can. Think about where you want to live, what kind of work you want to do, what work life balance you would like, how much you want to make, how much time to travel you would like... Be detailed and thorough.

Chapter 3

Goal Setting

The namesake for this book stems from the beginning of my own healing journey. A series of goals I titled, "Project Get Your Shit Together." Shortly after the meltdown of a relationship and subsequent breakup I found myself comatose on my couch smoking weed non-stop. Literally smoking to the point where I felt nothing but the hot air burning against my throat. No high, no buzz. I did this for weeks.

When this cycle finally ended, I knew I needed to get my life in order. I had experienced goal setting in the past, but this is when I really refined my method. There are key cornerstones that I believe are essential, but your method for implementing them is for you to decide. I will lay forth exactly what I did to reach my goals and you decide for yourself what suits you.

Write them down

This is absolute first step you must take is deciding what is you want to accomplish. That may sound obvious, but you would be surprised how many people have absolutely no clue what it is they really want. So, when you are through with this section, put the book down, sit, think and reflect on what it is you want.

SPECIFICALLY.

Make Them Positive.

Before you get too far into the details, one key component to your goals is making them positive statements. Too often our goals are made in a negative light. The difference is subtle, but critical. For instance, *"I'm tired of being broke, I don't want to be poor anymore."* Nothing wrong with wanting more wealth in life, but the language used in these statements is focused on the negative. Rather reframe this idea into, "I want to have abundance of wealth or I want to have financial freedom."

We attract what we set our minds on. "I'm tired of being single, I don't want to be alone anymore." Single, alone, these are what your mind fixates on. This is the state it will create. Another chapter will be dedicated to this specifically, but just to plant the seed in your head, your mind is not always your ally. There is a voice in your head that is constantly guiding you, telling you how you think, how you feel, what's good, what's bad. It is a voice and just like every voice you have ever encountered in your life it has the power and is often quite deceptive.

"If there is no enemy within, the enemy outside can do us no harm,"
– African Proverb

Here is a list of some common goals in both the positive and negative light. See if any of these pertain to you and if not, how might these ideas relate to goals you would like to accomplish?

Negative	Positive
I'm tired of being overweight.	I want to be fit.
I'm sick of being stuck in this small town.	I want to live in a community where I feel I have value.
I hate my job.	I want a career where I am fulfilled and appreciated.

I'm sick of being addicted to cigarettes.	I want to be free of my nicotine dependency.
I hate I never follow through on my dreams.	I want to finish what I start.

Be Specific

The next component in creating goals that will transform them into reality is making them specific. Often our goals go unaccomplished is because they are too vague. Even if we do accomplish them, sometimes they are so ambiguous that the changes are barely recognizable. Lets' go back to the example of weight loss. Say your positive goal is, "I want to lose weight." Great start, but not clear enough. With this in your head you could hit the gym everyday, maybe cutback on junk food a little bit and drop a few pounds. You look in the mirror and notice no change, the frustration enters. You technically accomplished your goal. You lost weight, just not quite what you are hoping for.

One of the missing components was being specific. Rather than, "I want to lose weight," a more specific and fulfilling goal may be, "I want to lose 30 pounds." Now you have changed your goal to something specific and measurable. This will help you in the next section about monitoring your progress. Here are some more examples about how to change a vague goal into a concrete specific goal

Vague	Specific
I want to travel.	I want to visit Madrid the spring.
I want to be wealthy.	I want to make at least sixty thousand dollars each year.
I want a partner.	I want someone who shares a similar lifestyle, similar beliefs and fulfills me.

Create a Plan for Action

You now have a positive specific goal, now is the time to create a specific actionable plan to put it in motion. Some goals will be simpler than others to create a plan. Weight loss? Go to the gym four times a week, go for a run three times, limit the number of calories consumed per day. Note that what you need to do is *simple*, but not necessarily easy. The hard part is staying consistent and following through. Without this component you will be like Sisyphus pushing a boulder up a mountain, only to watch it roll all the way back down.

The larger or more ambitious your goal is, the more complicated your plan will need to be. Starting a business, shifting career paths, finding more fulfilling relationships, are goals that may be more complicated when it comes to the actions you need to take. Especially when you are lacking experience the path might not always be clear.

If you are unsure of what you need to do that's okay. Anyone who has set forth on ventures like these knew what to do from the start. What you need to do is consider your opportunities and take small steps.

Be Timely

Another critical component for your goals is to give them a specific time frame. If you leave your goals in the realm of someday or the future, I can almost guarantee they will never happen. One of the most common bucket-list goals I hear from people is they want to go skydiving, *someday*. Someday they want to know what it's like to leap from a plane towards the earth. Someday.

Let me tell you this is the easiest life goal you could possibly accomplish. Presuming you live near any reasonably populated areas I guarantee there is a skydiving operation within an hour of you. You could go accomplish this life goal *today*.

People more often than not don't though. I've literally offered dozens of people to go on the weekend when they bring it up and every time I was met with excuses. Not a good time, not enough money, not this weekend, but some other time. Someday, the future and some better time are nothing, but procrastination and excuses.

Understand that there is a time and place for everything. Sometimes you are going to be too overwhelmed with responsibilities to dedicate much towards yourself. In that respect show yourself some compassion. It's easy for us to get down on ourselves and get discouraged if we don't feel like we are moving forward. Sometimes slow gradual change is the best we can do and that's just fine. Be mindful of your most stressful times but know there will never be a time when everything is convenient. There is no perfect moment or time when the stars will align, and everything will be right to start your dreams. You need to make the time, you need to your moment.

Don't fall into the trap of letting your dreams live in a fantasy. Give yourself a time frame to accomplish a goal and stick to it. You've been dreaming about writing a book? Give yourself a year and get it done. You want to go back to school? See when the deadlines are and get your application in.

Track Your Progress

The next step that will ensure success on your journey is to track your progress. Doing so will help you in many ways. First, most goals that are truly rewarding require a tremendous amount of time and effort. As such, it may take a long time to reach the end.

Tracking your progress allows you to take pride and feel accomplished while you are on the journey. I am a huge advocate for using whiteboards to track your progress. They allow you to see all the work you've done and ensure you are doing what you need to. I have a whiteboard in my office with many components.

I have my weekly list of to do items. Working out, writing classes, attending networking events. Having everything prominently displayed lets me see what I've done and what is left to do. I highly suggest adopting the same practice. The other important aspect of tracking your progress is holding yourself accountable.

Hold Yourself Accountable

As you go on journey you will find many roadblocks and hiccups along the way. We can only control ourselves, but circumstances outside your control are going to impact you no matter what. As such, there is a fine line to walk when it comes to holding yourself accountable.

Sometimes life is going to throw you curveballs. Your boss will hold you late, a big project will take up weeks of your semester, your position will be terminated, and you need to find new work. In these moments you might not have time for your goals. You were crushing the gym, but now there's no time for it. It's important to be flexible and allow yourself slack when your life gets turned upside down. Allow yourself some compassion. Take a night off, relax with a movie or comforting tv show, get yourself a nice meal. Part of finding balance is allowing ourselves to enjoy what fulfills our other needs.

On the flipside, also be ready to call yourself on your bullshit. Did you really have no time to go to the gym? Was every second of your time occupied. Did you spend time watching TV, going out with friends, scrolling through whatever app on your phone? If you want change, you are going to have to make sacrifices along the way.

Allow Room for Errors.

Finally allow yourself to make mistakes. You aren't going to do everything perfect right away. That's okay. We only truly experience failure when we quit. If you start and fail and start and fail and at the end you keep going, that's a success. Follow these steps and know that you can accomplish whatever you set your mind to.

Challenge: Write down a goal, make it specific, make it a positive statement, create a plan of action, give yourself a time frame to accomplish it. Begin today.

Chapter 4

Poor Goals

New Years Resolutions

Every year come January first people look to change their world. New Year's Resolutions. Hit the gym, no more smoking, cut out fast food. Millions of good intentions, all mostly doomed to fail. Some people truly do put down the pack of cigarettes New Year's Day and never look back. The overwhelming majority, however, attempt their new goal for a little while, quickly burn out and put it off until "next year." There are many issues with New Year's resolutions, but I'll surmise a few issues with them and let you mull it over. Notice how they may or may not apply to your circumstances.

One issue behind these goals is they are fueled on "motivation." Motivation, inspiration, aspiration, however you want to describe this feeling of excitement and energy. You're full of life ready to take on this new journey and be the you you've always dreamed of. You hit the gym, go hard, leave tired, but excited about how you're on your way. Rather quickly though, the excitement fades, your motivation drops and now your tank is running on empty.

Real change occurs through discipline. Going to the gym even when you don't *feel* like it. You said you would go three times a week, it's Thursday, that means now until Saturday you need to go. That's the agreement you committed to, that's the path you are on. Motivation can be your ally some days. After a podcast or a friend that inspires you, motivation may move you to chase your own dreams. Sometimes like a summer romance, it may be a fleeting ally and then depart you. If you want real change, and to actually accomplish your dreams, you will have to fuel your own fires and not rely on outside motivation.

The second problem with NYR is they are often on the backend of procrastination. We all have our dreams and goals. We know our bad habits that need to stop. We know what we need to do, yet we procrastinate dealing with these problems. Sometimes moments of have clarity strike. You realize what it is needed to be done, but right around this time period, procrastination takes over. Say you know you've become over dependent on caffeine. It's really time to take a break from your morning lattes. But it's the holidays, a time to treat yourself, you'll just have them now until the new year and then right after that you're going to start doing what you need to.

The time to do anything is now. That moment of clarity is a lot rarer than you might imagine. You never know how long it will be before it comes back to you. The time to change is not a week from now, after New Year's or after some other arbitrary date. Do what you need to now. Time is precious.

Think on what it means to procrastinate these things and the consequences of such actions. If you truly believe you would be happier and more well-off losing weight, quitting your addictions, starting that new project or whatever it is, why would you put it off? Why would you delay your happiness? Wouldn't you rather have it sooner rather than later?

Imagine your toilet is busted and you call a plumber. They say they can be there this afternoon or next week. You'd obviously want them to come this afternoon. Well your life is the broken toilet. You are the plumber and it's up to you to fix it. No one will do it for you. Your loved ones may wish you the best, may offer support, but the person who will work the absolute hardest for you is yourself. You have the most stake in your own happiness. Be your own ally.

Diets

Diets are also poor goals. At least dieting in the sense of it being a temporary change. You're gonna go on a "cleanse". Nothing but fresh veggie juices for the next month. That's what the latest fitness guru told you. Your neighbor did it and now they're down twenty pounds. Tried and true.

You may very well find "success" through dieting. You may lose the weight you've been fixated on for years. It may work, for a time. The problem, however, is that diets are temporary. They are not sustainable and when they end, most people go back to their old ways.

They go back to eating the same foods they always did. They stop exercising. The weight comes back. I really enjoy using weight loss and fitness as examples for a few different reasons. One in the western world they are fairly common issues that impact a large amount of people. In most developed countries obesity is the norm. The other reason is that they are simple and straightforward.

While dieting is a poor goal, an effective alternative is a total shift in your nutrition. Choosing to incorporate vegetables into all your meals. Committing to having a salad once a day, limiting or eliminating the amount of processed foods, cutting out useless poisons like soda. Often people go on diets because it will net a large return in a short amount of time.

If you go on a purely liquid diet you will certainly lose a lot of weight. This is not sustainable though. Rather than going for a quick fix or a temporary change, switching your nutritional lifestyle will give you lasting change.

When you start eating healthier and consistently your body will reach a new normal. It will find balance and homeostasis. If you are able to detach from a number on a scale or the amount of time it takes to reach your desired weight you will find tranquility and peace.

Personally, I had the opposite experience in relation to weight. As a teenager I was constantly underweight and insecure about my size. Finally, in my twenties I decided enough was enough and that I would bulk up.

I did my research, started counting my calories, worked out and ate. I ate so much. From the moment I woke up until the end of the day I pretty much at every two to three hours. Daily I would drink protein shakes with 1300 to 1600 calories. I did this for years and went from 145 to 175 pounds.

I was proud of my accomplishment, but it was absolute hell on my body. I was constantly bloated and uncomfortable. If I traveled or went camping, I would shed weight immediately. In order to sustain this body, I essentially had to be within two hours of my fridge. Eventually, I had enough.

I let go of having the desire to have this bulky physique. I decided that I would eat what made my body feel healthy. I would work out in a way that was sustainable. Whatever my body ended up looking like would be it.

Now I feel better than I ever did. I don't obsess over what a number on a scale says. I don't determine my value based on how much weight I can bench. Find the nutrition your body requires, find modes of exercise that resonates with you, and your body will come to its natural state. Temporary diets are poor goals. Long term sustainable shifts in your daily nutrition are great. Work towards creating goals that are sustainable and worthwhile.

Chapter 5

Tidy Your Space

One of the simplest steps that will clear your mind is to clean up your living space. Most children groan when they are told to make their bed. It's easy to ask, "why do I have to make it if I'm just going to mess it up tonight?" I've met many twenty and thirty-year-old's that share this attitude as well. If this is your outlook I have to ask, why do anything then?

Why do your laundry? Why do the dishes? Why brush your teeth in the morning if they're just gonna get dirty throughout the day? Most people would agree that you brush your teeth to keep them healthy, to keep them looking good, and to make your breath tolerable for the rest of us. No one is making a case against brushing your teeth. Why not take the care you would for your teeth and apply it to the rest of your life? Starting with where you live.

Your external environment is a reflection of your internal headspace. If you live in a chaotic mess of unkempt laundry, dirty dishes and disorder, mentally you will be equally cluttered. Cleaning your physical environment simultaneously frees your mind.

The biggest proponents against regular cleaning stem their argument from a standpoint of laziness or not wanting to do more work. A shadow in our mind tells us it's not worth it, that cleaning is more work than it's worth. This is one of those mental tricks that in fact creates the opposite reality.

There are basically two ways you can go about cleaning. One method is to let a mess pile up day after day. Your sink becomes over-flowing, your bathroom tiles have turned a shade of green brown, your bedroom has become a blackhole of clutter for which you have no idea where anything is. A day finally comes when you are tired of this disaster and go about cleaning this mess. Hours are spent reorganizing, scrubbing and putting everything back in its proper place. This whole process is unnecessary and now you've actually programmed your mind to look at cleaning in a negative way.

Now when you think of cleaning, you imagine this multi-hour-long ordeal that you have to get through. This association will cause you to do everything in your power to avoid doing this again. We are drawn to what's comfortable and avoid discomfort at all cost. This is our nature. The cycle repeats. Dishes pile up, the laundry doesn't get put away, on and on until the day comes that you, your partner, your parent, whomever decides this mess needs to be handled and you do it all over again.

Fortunately, it's quite simple to escape this unpleasant cycle. If your place is already a mess, you'll have to give it a good scrub down, but once your place is all neat and tidy, all you need is some active maintenance. What should you do instead? I would suggest doing small bits of daily cleaning, with the occasional deep clean.

What does daily cleaning look like? Make your bed, do your dishes, put your laundry away, sweep, wipe the counters, simple quick easy little daily maintenances that will keep your home clean and organized.

If you are used to not cleaning up it can be hard to imagine how different things would be if you did. You've survived this far in life without making your bed, why start now? Like many things you will learn in this book you must accept that if you want change, you need to change your behaviors. Often with self-help books, the promise is that by reading through the book you will come to a new understanding and life will better without actually doing anything. I'm telling you that change only happens through action. Concrete actionable steps are required. For many this will require a growing-up, a moving towards a more professional lifestyle.

Let's use the analogy of being a professional in the context of environments. Say for instance a hotel. How would you feel if you entered a hotel room and the bed was in complete disarray? Even if house-keeping had gone through, replaced the dirty sheets with clean ones, how would you feel with an unmade bed? Dirty towels on the floor, used shampoo bottles in the shower still wet from the previous guest. Most people wouldn't be happy, to say the least. Most would be furious and outraged. If you wouldn't tolerate a dirty hotel room, why is this acceptable at your home? Treat yourself and your home with the same due diligence and care you would expect if you stayed at a hotel.

Another funny instance is that often if people have guests staying at their place. They'll give them fresh sheets and a nice made bed. Most people do that without any thought or concerns about how much "work" it is. Yet day after day, they are content to come home to a mess for themselves.

It's so easy to put in extra effort for others, but not ourselves. I challenge you now to change this behavior and see how far it takes you. Go at it slowly too. You don't need to suddenly change everything in your life, but one of the most impactful ones you can do on a daily basis is simply making your bed every morning. It takes less than a minute. Pull the sheets up, put the pillows in the right place, done.

Beyond that little things like sweeping after cooking, taking out the trash or recycling when it's full, dusting when it's visible, etc. that will make your life easier and your home more respectable. Think about the difference you feel when you visit a friend's home and it's immaculate over your buddy who never cleans up after themselves. Living for the approval of other is something I highly discourage and will go into detail later, but in this situation it's worth noting. A clean home shows the world you are responsible, dependable and can take care of yourself. A messy home says you're either a slob or a child that needs to be looked after. Who do you want to be?

These are simple little daily steps you can take that will keep your place clean, keep you from having to deep clean, and will make your life a thousand times easier. You actually end up doing less work than you would normally so if you're in the mindset of not wanting to do more work, this is actually less work. Afterwards there are a few bigger things that you will have to tackle on a less regular basis.

With the bigger chores I would certainly recommend having a regularly scheduled time for this. Say every Wednesday before bed is when you do your laundry. You could make the last Sunday of every month your time to go through and give your bathroom some tender loving care. If having a rigid schedule doesn't serve you or your schedule shifts too often to not have that as a practical option, don't sweat it. Find a system that works for you.

As before with daily maintenance, the more regularly you practice these chores, the less work you will end up ultimately doing. Think about the amount of time it takes to clean your bathroom after one month of cleaning, compared to three months.

Finally, some other steps you can take to simplify your life is creating systems of organization. This will highly vary among person to person. Each room of your home/apartment/tiny home/van dwelling will differ in terms of its' needs and requirements. This is certainly an area where I have some rooms more organized than others, higher standards for some, and there's really no right or wrong answer. What I offer here are some of the systems I use, some systems I think work efficiently. Take it or leave it if it benefits you.

Simple ways to organize your home.

- Alphabetize your spices. It will save you so much time when cooking to have everything listed from A to Z. It will also likely end up saving you money. At one point I had three massive jars of crushed red pepper flakes because I would check a recipe, see I needed them and wasn't sure if I already had some. Empty your spice rack, put them in alphabetical order, put them back in the right place when you're finished using them. It'll take five minutes and I promise it'll be worth it.
- Alphabetize your movies/games/vinyls. Now this may no longer be entirely relevant as we move into the digital age, however if you still have DVDs, Blu-Rays, and game disks I highly recommend putting them in alphabetical order so when there's something specific you want you know where it is.
- Put your clothes in drawers. One for t-shirts, underwear, socks, etc. Nothing complicated about it just do it.
- Organize cleaning supplies. Under your bathroom sink put your bathroom cleaning supplies. Do the same in your kitchen.
- Organize your hobbies. As an avid outdoorsman I have a few different bins for each of them specifically. I have a bin for my snowboard gear, for my camping gear, for climbing, for diving and for surfing. Maybe you aren't outdoorsy, but you

could easily apply the same concept for art supplies.
- Organize your kitchen. Have a cabinet for dishes, pots and pans, silverware, etc. Have a designated spot for everything and when you're finished using it put it back. We lose so much time fumbling where to find what we are looking for.

This list could go on and on, but I think you get the general gist of what I'm getting at. Organize your living space. You'll be rewarded with a more beautiful area to call home, an easier and more functionable space, and I would argue most importantly a decluttered mind free of the unnecessary added weight of a disorganized mess.

"Clutter is the physical manifestation of unmade decisions fueled by procrastination."
– Christina Scalise

Chapter 6

Feeling Ready

One habit that keeps many of us stuck in place is not wanting to start something until we're ready. We are all guilty of this. Know that you are not alone and there is no need to be hard on yourself. At some point we must all overcome this tendency and in order to do so we need to understand the root cause. At its' core, this habit is driven by our fear of failure.

The trap you may find yourself in is never ending preparation. You read one self-help book and it was great, but you heard about another and you want to read that before you start your journey. Maybe you've found some guru on YouTube and you want to go through all of their content before you begin. Perhaps there's a podcast, a seminar, a class you're taking, whatever your outlet, you may be using these excuses to procrastinate starting.

With any new endeavor you will never be able to prepare enough. There's no amount of books you can read, videos you can watch or lessons to learn that will fully prepare you. Nothing will eliminate these feelings of doubt for your readiness. If you are hoping for that here, you are going to be disappointed. It will never happen. What will free you and bring you to the state that you can start is by going out and actually doing the work.

You will make mistakes. You will fail. This is great. Although your instincts and mental chatter may be telling you that you aren't ready, you need to be the stronger voice and say you're going to do it anyway. You need to be ok that you will fail. There is nothing wrong with failure. In fact, failure is the only real road to success. I implore you to dive straight in.

Maybe you've dreamed of being a standup comedian. You grew up watching it for years, you listen to podcasts of your favorites daily, it's all you've ever wanted. You always had a knack for making for friends laugh. As this dream became more real you started writing down your bits. Maybe you've got a few minutes worth of content. If that's you right now sign up for an open mic night. You might be thinking you want to tweak it a little more, it's not quite ready, you're not quite confident enough to speak in front of crowds. Do it anyways. You can never prepare enough, your jokes will never be good enough, you won't wake up one day with the fear of speaking in front of people magically gone. It will never happen. The only way out is through. Go out and just do it.

You want to write a book? Put this one down and start now. Seriously. Get out a notebook, get on your computer, pull up notes on your phone and write something. Anything. Write an outline. Write your stream of consciousness. Get something down and just get the ball rolling.

In physics there is a principle of motion. The hardest part of moving an object is the initial instigating moment. Take a car as an example. A car in place takes a tremendous amount of gas and energy to get it moving. Once you start accelerating it remains in motion with just a little bit of energy. We operate the same way. With new habits and challenges, it takes a lot to get things started at the beginning. Once you've started though it's much easier to keep going.

I know it's scary. I know it's uncomfortable. I know how much resistance you may be feeling and how difficult it is to overcome it. I know. I was there and I still grapple with those feelings to this day.

After I completed Yoga Teacher Training, I spent months diving into my practice. I was a "certified teacher" but in no way did I feel ready to teach a class. I dove into books learning the history of yoga, the philosophy of the Upanishads, Bhagavad Gita and other sacred texts. I studied and practiced. Months later the day came when I finally sat down to teach my first class and I still felt beyond inept. It felt clunky and weird. So difficult to remember the sequence I had created, how to get into each pose, what cuing to use. It was undoubtably awkward, but I did it. I learned and I grew. Even after teaching classes on a weekly basis, now having years of personal experience in the practice I still feel like a beginner. There are still doubts and worries that arise. What keeps me grounded and moving forward is focusing on what I can control, doing my best and pushing through. The best in any medium share this sentiment.

Feeling like an imposter is something we all have to overcome. Every person who has ever done anything worthwhile and has a shred of humility felt this way and may never truly overcome it. Ringo Starr, legendary Beatle's drummer, rock icon, famously admits to throwing up before their shows for decades. If one of the world's most iconic performers gets stage fright before his shows, you are allowed to feel uncomfortable before your endeavor.

It's ok to have those feelings. What important is how you respond. You have to do it anyways.

Whatever your chosen field, you need to face your fears and push through. No one can do it but you. This is where you have to save yourself and learn how to fly on your own. You will stumble along the way. Mistakes will be made, you may be embarrassed, you may be laughed at, but your critics would never have the courage to elevate themselves the way you would. Let their critiques be your fuel. Transform their negative energy into your own fuel and soar higher to be that person you always dreamed of.

Challenge: Make one step towards your dream today. Nothing gigantic or overwhelming, simply do something that gets you one step closer to the person you want to be. If your dream is to lose weight, go walk around your neighborhood. If you want to write a book, put this one down, grab a pen and paper or your laptop and write a page, write a paragraph. Take a tangible action that moves you forward.

Chapter 7

Ask For Help

Our culture has perpetuated this backwards notion that asking for help is a sign of weakness. This toxic idea needs to be eradicated from the world. There is nothing wrong with asking for help. In fact, it takes a tremendous amount of courage and self-awareness to do so. To know that you're not capable enough, not educated enough or simply lack experience in your chosen endeavor, takes a tremendous amount of humility and honest introspection.

It seems all too common that we have expectations that we should be masters or perfect at our craft immediately. Especially for beginners, this makes no sense. If you just started writing, just started practicing piano, went rock-climbing for the first time, you are not going to good at it. There is nothing wrong or embarrassing about being bad at something you have no experience in. The good news is that when you start at the bottom you can only go up.

When it comes to your craft, you have two options. You can grind it out on your own, stumbling and failing all by yourself, or you can dramatically improve your abilities by asking mentors for help. Think of the stubborn man who enters a hardware store looking for a specific part with no knowledge of the layout of the store. Now the employee up front asks if he needs any assistance and due to some misplaced pride or shame in asking for help, he says no. For the next half-hour he wanders each isle aimlessly until he finds what he's looking for. Figured it out all by himself what a man. Or he simply could have told the employee what he needed, been guided to the correct isle and have left in a few minutes.

Behind the charade of the do-it-yourself man's man attitude is fear. It is a fear of being seen as incompetent, a fear of not being enough, it is toxic fear and it is beyond unnecessary. When you break these fears down, they are so ridiculous and illogical it is laughable. Knowing that your fears originate from baseless space may not take away all of their impact, but it can dampen its effect allowing you to persevere.

Take the hardware store example. This man has never stepped foot in this door, has no knowledge of the layout, no frame of reference. Why then would he have any knowledge of the store? Is there some hardware store genes passed along the Y-chromosome that should have imbued him with the gift of hardware store omniscience?

Spelling it out this way seems ridiculous, but we get caught up in these patterns so often. We get discouraged, we say we can't do things, when we've barely ever tried or have any experience. You really want to write. You've had ideas in your head for years of the perfect story. You finally sit down, pour your heart and soul into it, it's finished. You share it with your friend and with a half-hearted smile they tell you what they liked. Seeing through their polite demeanor you ask for honest feedback and they lay it out for you. It's bad. Not only is it bad, it's not great and at best it would make nice kindling for a fire.

What did you expect? Your first work was going to be a masterpiece. You're going to go from sales rep at a marketing firm to Shakespeare on your first attempt? Your first work, your first few works are going to suck. Take a minute, let that sink in and accept it. Know that it may take a while for these ideas to resonate. For now, hold them and simply play with the idea as we go further into detail.

Once you come to terms with that though you can free yourself of the burden of creating something quality right away. Your first video sucked, your first song was trash, first poem was laughable? Good, it should be. Now keep going. Keep refining, ask for feedback, be willing to learn and if you are fortunate enough to have people willing to help you ask for help.

Mentors will skyrocket your progress. You can stumble and fall, figure things out the hard way, but you can save yourself a lot of time and heartache by finding people to help guide you. They can tell you pitfalls that were massive time sinks that led nowhere. They can give you strategies that worked well. Their insight will give you direction and clarity.

Teachers can cut down your learning curve and guide you towards a path of success. It depends on the person/industry/area of focus, but more often than not if you are a good student, they will help you. Teachers love sharing their experience with eager students. There is an immense satisfaction sharing your craft, wisdom and insights with the next generation.

As such there are a few qualities that make for good students that are important if you hope to have a mentor guide you. One is the beginner's mindset. When you are studying under a teacher, assume you know nothing.

Even if they are starting at the basics, even if you already have experience, keep your mouth shut and listen.

While I attended the American Alpine Institute for mountain-guiding-training, one of my classmates constantly would interrupt with his own opinions. He would go on about what he did in the field, or what he read in books, or what he heard online. His incessant chatter constantly disrupted the flow of our exercises, drove the rest of us students crazy and even had to be told not to interrupt by the instructors. Shut up and listen.

Pay attention. That might sound obvious, but there is nothing more irritating explaining something in depth to have someone ask a question about what you just went over. Now there's nothing wrong with asking questions to clarify confusion. This is actually a sign that you are paying attention, however if you ask me what the second point of being a good student is, I'm not gonna be very happy with you. Listen, pay attention.

Next, do your work and be dependable. Amazingly, more than being talented, knowledgeable about a craft or experienced, being dependable is a rare quality. If you show up and do your work consistently, you will be miles ahead of your competition. I would much rather work with someone who has no experience and will do everything I ask, then someone with years of experience I can't rely on. Again, it seems simple, but often those with "talent" get cocky and arrogant. There's a tendency to not put in the work or slack off. They let their ego's run amuck and think they're the best and that's all that matters. No one is that talented. There is no task where talent overcomes hard work. What's often labeled as talent, more often than not, is simply the result of countless hours spent honing that craft.

Of course, there are a myriad of other qualities that make for a good student. My intent is not to bombard you with every possible example, but to highlight the essentials so that you can find mentors and have a fulfilling relationship with them. In summation.

Ask for help. It takes more courage to ask for help and your progress will skyrocket for it. Have a beginner's mindset. Be willing to learn and relearn. Say you go over a point you've already covered, good, it just reinforces that idea and makes it stronger in your mind. Pay attention. Listen. Ask questions to clarify, but if you aren't paying attention, you're wasting their time and yours. Mentors owe you nothing and if you can't show your appreciation by listening, they will soon be gone from your life.

Do you work and be dependable. Hard work beats talent every time, period.

Chapter 8

Focus On What You Can Control

It often seems like our lives are at the whims of the universe. We feel trapped and restricted by our circumstances. Whether that's our financial situation, our careers, our bodies, it seems as though we were dealt unfair cards for which we have no say.

Beyond this is the greater context of the world we live in. The town you grew up in, the country you live or even this very day and age we are alive in. All these circumstances seem to impose restrictions on our lives.

Everything that was just described will be important to your journey, but those factors hold much less power than you might imagine. Overwhelmingly, spending time worrying or complaining about your circumstances does nothing. All you end up doing is wasting precious energy and time to no end.

I grew up with severe depression and anxiety. I felt fundamentally flawed. I internalized a lot of it as there being something inherently wrong with me. A built-in manufactured default. Most of my life I believed I was broken and that was it. I would shift the blame between myself and my parents more than anything else.

Some days I would think I was a loser, a quitter, I was weak, and it was my fault. Other times I would push the responsibility off, especially on to my father. My thoughts would sing a tune along the lines, *"I'm anti-social, but he never taught me how to be social. I'm not a man, but he never taught me how to be one."* I was broken, but I was made that way.

Nature and nurture are two difficult concepts when it comes to who we are. Are we the product of our environment, our genetics, our upbringing, our class, or our country? This debate has lasted as long as human history. While they both played a role in your own development, I'm here to tell you obsessing over them gets you nowhere.

Regardless of why you are the way you are, what's more important is what you plan to do about it. In the instance of my social anxiety I faced a crossroads. I could have decided that because of my genetics or the way I was raised I was anti-social and that would be the end of it. Any hopes of making friends or finding a partner I could have been thrown out the window. That was an option. Believe me, I chose that mindset for many years. For years and years, I chose defeatist victimhood.

Fortunately, that was not my fate. Through trial and error, I made progress. I read books on socializing and making friends. Dale Carnegie's *How to Win Friends and Influence People* I could not recommend enough to everyone. Beyond that I read books from CIA and FBI operatives on body language. I read dozens of books on psychology. An endless series of podcasts and videos online of "experts" on socializing.

I studied for years and would make efforts to grow outside of my limited shell. In college, I joined a million clubs that never seemed to lead anywhere. Never seemed to make lasting friendships.

Looking back, I'd say that every step was necessary. I needed the books to open my eyes to ideas I wasn't aware of. Maintaining eye contact, body language, ques, active listening. Studies give different percentages, but the overwhelming consensus amongst social scientists is that the majority of our communication is non-verbal.

Meaning the words we use and verbally speaking are really the tip of the iceberg in terms of communication.

Your circumstances are out of your control. You had no say in the family you were born into, where and how you were raised. Some people get lucky and are financially well off, some had parents that were great mentors, others quite the exact opposite.

Ignore your circumstances, focus on what you can control. You want to write movies or tv shows do it. Do it every day and get good at it. Hammer on your craft until you are a master.

Robert Greene in his novel *Mastery* postulated the idea that it takes 10,000 hours to become a master at something. That number can seem big and scary but let me break it down more tangibly. If you spent 40 hours a week working on your craft, at the end of a year that's 2080 hours. So in less than five years you have become a master. I understand that's also a big commitment, but how many people do that for jobs they hate for years or for their whole lives. Switching priorities to long-term fulfillment means sacrificing temporary pleasures for a greater reward. The road may be longer, but in the end, you will live a life uncompromised and by your own design. Isn't that worth some minor inconveniences?

Keep in mind too that you don't need to be a master to be compensated. There are plenty of "mediocre" writers, actors, musicians, etc. that are still paid for their work. Money isn't the only important factor when considering how to spend your time, but it certainly is a consideration.

Your time is your most precious commodity. Think about how you spend it. I will also add that there are no correct answers here.

In the field of writing one of my favorite authors Steven Pressfield says he writes for about 4-5 hours a day. Other writers go extreme length of 10-12. Personally, I work best in about 3-hour chunks before my mind needs to move on to something else. That offers me time to dedicate to my other interests, hobbies and jobs.

Some people will want to master their craft as soon as possible, others are more content taking a longer road. There are pros and cons to both. Decide for yourself what is in your best interests. Be ruthlessly honest.

Challenge: Make a timeline for your week. Fill your days completely breakfast, commuting, work, TV, friends, hobbies, etc. every single detail of the day. Now see where you have gaps in your time and where you could add time for your new habit. Designate a specific time for it and stick to it.

Chapter 9

Worrying About Future, Regretting the Past, Staying Present

Worry is by far one of the most insidious time wasters. It zaps our energy and immobilizes us into inaction. Worry takes many forms shapes and sizes. While all these subjects could be given their own chapters, I feel as though the ideas governing each are intertwined and so grouped them together for this section.

The Past

Regretting the past is such a prison to be trapped in. I can say from first-hand experience I spent years and years in a state constantly feeling an overwhelming sense of guilt and remorse over my past actions. First, I want to say that if you are in such a state chronically, I completely understand. In some ways regret is "good" in that it shows you have a conscience. You know your past behaviors were not acceptable and that upsets you. That is actually a good state considering how many people do the same and yet feel no sense of shame or remorse.

The problem with regret happens when it becomes overbearing and doesn't lead to change. Countless times I remember pissing people off, being rude or violent, disrespectful, I caused while drunk. The next day I would come to, learn of my transgressions and be profoundly mortified. I would apologize and beg for forgiveness. I would say how sorry I was and be filled with a tremendous sense of guilt and shame. If this were a one and done situation, that might be appropriate, but this pattern existed for many, many years.

It took me so long to realize that what really matters in these situations is learning. Learn from your mistakes. You don't like how you behaved? You're upset with how you handled a situation? Well the thing with the past is it's over. The past is set in stone. You get one shot with this life, no do-overs, no repeats, just once. The thing with your life though is that it's long. While you can't change your past, you can change your future.

For me, it came with drinking and not wanting to be that person anymore. I didn't want to start fights, didn't want to send inappropriate texts to people, didn't want all the chaos that resulted from me being out of control. I stopped. Now those problems are over. I caused a lot of destruction, severed many friendships and relationships because of how I acted on alcohol, but that is no longer me. That is no longer my identity.

One of the ways regrets trap us is they make us think we are tied to this identity. Regret convinces us we are the mistakes of our past. We're the fuckup, the drunk, the loner, the loser, the fat kid, the skinny kid... You are not your past. Let me reiterate that so it sinks in. **You are not your past.** Part of being human is making mistakes. Some of us make bigger mistakes than others, but no one gets through life unscathed. You will make mistakes along the way. You can have the best of intentions, thoroughly research and plan to the best of your abilities and still fail. That's ok. Take the lessons you need and move forward.

The Future

Worrying about the future is another one of our most fruitless habits. Sometimes it feels as if we have no say in the matter. Our worries and fears seem to consume us. Much like many of the other negative thought patterns I have illustrated to you, this is another you will have to overcome. While we don't have the ability to control the future, we do have a say in how we feel about it.

When I tell you that it is pointless to worry about the future, I must clarify that thinking about the future is useful. Having foresight, being intentional with your actions and being aware of potential scenarios you may encounter is very beneficial to you. There is a difference however between contemplating the possible future and actively dreading it.

In many ways I have tried to impart knowledge on how to empower you. I want to show you and teach you how to take control of your destiny. Ultimately the reality we are all subject to is that the universe has the final say in how our lives play out. We get to choose how we think about our circumstances, how we behave with our feelings and the actions we take. That's up to us. The rest is out of your control.

For those anxious at that notion who crave control, my only condolence and way I hope to ease your stress is to let go of your desire for security. Easier said than done. My practice when it comes to the future has a few components I want to share with you. Hopefully they resonate, regardless just play with these ideas for a moment if you will.

One strategy I use is to imagine all possible outcomes. Let's take the example of applying for a job. Say you sent in your application, they loved what they saw and now you are preparing for your interview.

For many, this is where their fears and worrying may arise. What if they don't like you? What if you're nervous? How should you dress? How are you going to answer questions? What if they ask questions you don't have answers to? On and on, fears have the uncanny ability to multiply and keep us paralyzed.

First, breath. Next if you are truly overcome with all these fears, I would recommend writing them all out and following them to their natural conclusions. How should I dress? Well you have the option to be very formal, suit and tie or a dress, something along those lines. Or maybe it's a casual environment where a button-up may suffice. Call ahead see what they recommend or go in before your interview and see what the environment is like.

Take your fears to their ends and you will be free of their cages. Afterwards think about what the outcomes of this meeting will be. Job interviews tend to be quite binary with a few exceptions. Outcome number one is your worst fear, they reject you. Nope, you weren't cutout for it, weren't experienced enough, didn't vibe with the interviewer, etc. For whatever reason you were denied the position.

Now while rejection can be undeniably disappointing, I would like to reframe how you might process this interaction. You may think, "I lost the job," when in reality you never had the job. You had an opportunity for a position and were rejected. Maybe it was because of how you handled the interview, maybe not. Maybe someone who was a friend of the interviewer applied and they passed on you. Maybe someone more qualified applied. Maybe your interviewer just split up with their significant other and wasn't present for your interview. This is why it's important to focus on what you can control and then be ok with whatever outcome may come to be.

"So far you have survived one hundred percent of your worst days. This too shall pass."
– Unknown

Staying Present

On the opposite end of regretting your past or worrying about the future is staying present. Here and now is all that will ever be. The past is over, the future is yet to be. To the spiritually minded, this concept is likely one you are familiar with, but to those not let me elaborate. We have no guarantees in life. You can take care of your body, check every box on your responsibilities list and a car accident could end it all tomorrow.

By cultivating a sense of presence we are able to find peace. We are able to focus on the tasks at hand and appreciate all we have. This is certainly easier said than done. Even being aware and intentional with all these ideas, I won't lie that I never worry about the future. Staying present is an intention you will have to make on a daily basis. The more you do it, the better you will get and the more rewarding your life will be for it.

Chapter 10

Self-Sabotage

One component to becoming the best version of ourselves is getting out of our own way. For some this problem will be worse than others, but everyone is likely familiar with some form of self-sabotage. Sometimes we are aware of what we are doing. We eat the foods we shouldn't, skip on practicing that instrument, stop applying for jobs. These moments in a way are easier to handle because they are conscious choices we make. The more difficult demons to tame are our unconscious acts of self-sabotage. Without any intention or planning, we often trip ourselves, get in our own way, and slow down our progress.

"The man who says he can, and the man who says he cannot... are both correct."
– Confucius

One thing that can be very hard starting out is believing in yourself. When all you are accustomed to is failure, thinking you will succeed is undoubtedly a challenge. Another classic axiom you likely will have heard is, "fake it till you make it." Both of these statements are true and compliment each other.

The difficult truth is that if there is a goal you are reaching for, a thing you want to accomplish, something you want to posses and you think you can't do it, you can't. Simply put. If you think you will fail, you will. It's easy in self-loathing to put yourself down and say I can't do it, when in the back of your mind your hoping for someone to tell you otherwise. Your coach to come give you a pep-talk, your parents to lift you up, your significant other to tell you to keep pushing through. For some reason it can be more comforting or more motivating when someone else tells you, you can do it then when you tell yourself. Some of you will be blessed with support of those around you and others will have to tough it out on their own, there are pros and cons to both of these situations.

On one hand, the support of those that care about you can be invaluable. To have people that stick with you and get you through your ups and downs is nothing but a real blessing. Robert Downey Jr has credited his wife with getting him sober when she gave him and ultimatum of her or drinking. There are numerous stories of loved ones who stuck with their partner when they were at their absolute lowest moments, climbed out of that pit together and were stronger for it. There are parents that stick with their children through drug addictions until they're clean. Coaches that go the extra mile to help their struggling athletes make it. Those are all wonderful scenarios. If you are blessed to be in that situation, I hope you feel some gratitude for the compassion that was shown your way. This won't be everyone's circumstance though. While from the outside it can seem much colder and harsher, not all is lost for those going through it alone.

For those that their partner left, their parents gave up on them or were never around, who didn't have close friends to help them through their lows, you are going to have to either sink or swim. Reality is either going to crush you down into nothing or you will have to rise up to the challenge. I know how punishingly difficult that may sound but trust me in that there is a silver-lining.

Above all else you will learn self-reliance. This immeasurable skill if you master it will truly set you free. True freedom in that your life, your circumstances and your well-being will be of your own creation.

For me, one instance where I truly had to figure it out on my own was my sobriety. Beyond a forum I subscribed to about quitting drink (reddit.com/r/stopdrinking for those curious, truly a wonderful corner of the internet) I was entirely on my own when it came to my sobriety. I knew no sober people. Didn't have older people that had quit drinking to turn to for advice. I had books on people that stopped drinking, podcasts, and other cyber resources, but that was it.

Learning how to socialize, learning how to have an identity as a non-drinker and not apologize for it, learning how to have fun, go to concerts, go to anything that traditionally involved drinking, I did on my own. In no way was it the most pleasant experience. If you can find people to help you do it great, but I knew no one. A big reason behind writing this book is my hopes that I can pass along some of the lessons I learned so others don't have to learn it the hard way. Even easing the learning curve would make me happy.

Many months of discomfort, awkwardness, growing pains and unpleasantness followed my early sobriety. Eventually through persistence I felt like I reached a place where I overcame it. Where alcohol really held no sway or influence in my life. I was "triumphant". Every day brings a new challenge and I'm well aware that all it would take is one drink to fall back to where I was. I stay humble and vigilant in that regard.

At the end of it I had a real sense of pride and accomplishment. There's nothing wrong with achieving a victory with others, but there is a different kind of satisfaction when you do it on your own.

For those of you who are dealing with your problems without support, know that it is a blessing not a curse. It is an entirely different thing to succeed with the help of others, not better or worse.

To those that still may be skeptical of that I'll illustrate a little further. If you had help along the way of your journey, the help you received may have acted more as a crutch and in some ways limited your potential for growth.

One classic metaphor describes a moth breaking out of a cocoon. As the moth struggles and writhes to break free of its' cage a passerby might be inclined to offer assistance. Cut open the cocoon and let the moth fly free. While clearly having nothing but kind intentions this act would actually doom the moth. The struggle to break free from the cocoon strengthens this critter's wings and without the struggle it would be too weak to fly. By intervening, they would actually doom the moth.

In that same regard if you need to solve something on your own and there's always a safety net or someone looking after you, you may never learn to fly. I can't tell you when and where this will apply. It's simply an idea to keep in your head.

As I've stated previously it takes a tremendous amount of courage to ask for help and if you have the opportunity take any help you can get. With some of your obstacles and likely the ones that are at the center of your spiritual growth I believe you will have to traverse it alone. Your teachers, friends, mentors can all help you along the way, but at some point, you are going to have to overcome your obstacles on your own. You will be the one that has to break through your own limiting narratives and overcome your own internal resistance. As Morpheus stated in the Matrix, "I can only show you the door, you're the one that has to walk through it…"

Chapter 11

Exercise

Our bodies were not designed for the world we are living in. We were not built to sit behind computer screens, in cars and on couches for the majority of our waking state. Due to our sedentary lifestyle, obesity has skyrocketed and become a pandemic. We need to move our bodies.

Personally, weight training was what initially brought me out of depression. Not that it cured all my problems, but it gave me control. In the throughs of depression, I felt there was no hope, no escape. I felt broken and doomed to be that way forever. Weightlifting cleared much of these negative thoughts in my head, made some of those voices quieter.

Months and years of training brought a physique I was proud of. This is another concept that is often posed as some vain awful quality. That to want to look good or be happy with your appearance is some terrible trait. This is absurd. There are countless studies that state good-looking people are paid more, have more job opportunities, more relationship opportunities, etc. It might not seem fair, you might not like that idea, but that is the world we live in.

While our world certainly tries to make us feel insecure about our appearance, we must also keep in mind there is only so much in our control. Much of the way we look is due to our genetic makeup, something forever out of our control. Aiming to be healthy, rather than fixated over an arbitrary number on a scale or size of clothing, is a much more achievable and healthy aim. We need to learn to accept where we are, while still be focused on where we need to go.

Beyond our outward appearance though, I advocate exercise mainly for our mental wellbeing. For our bodies and minds to function healthily we need to exercise. I could end this chapter there. However, I want to dispel some ideas as well as give you options.

Exercise is unique for everyone. What resonates and what doesn't, we are all unique. For this reason, I highly encourage everyone to experiment with different form of exercise to find the one that speaks to you.

Personally, most of my exercise now stems from yoga. When I discovered the practice, it resonated with me physically, emotionally and spiritually. I was absolutely captivated and began dedicating most of my life to the tradition. As such, weightlifting fell by the wayside. I still weightlift occasionally, but nowhere near to the degree I did in the past. I am forever grateful for how it pulled me out of depression, but now it doesn't serve me in the same way it used to.

For many, weightlifting and the gym is their focus. The challenge speaks to them, calls them and that's wonderful. Others are runners, climbers, bikers, swimmers, etc. Many are a combination and that is also great. Doing the same workouts over and over can actually lead to injury if you are not getting adequate rest. Mixing up your routines will keep it fresh and interesting, promote more muscles groups and be better for you in the long run.

Go out and experiment. If you truly have no experience with any forms of exercise you have several options. First, I would look to your friends and family. Do you have friends that go to the gym that could take you?

If that's not possible, go to a gym and take a class. Box gyms often have free trial memberships, opportunities to try a personal trainer, group classes where you can learn with others. The same is true at yoga studios, climbing gyms, outdoor groups for running and biking.

Exercise was the very first step for me on my healing journey. It's what initially brought me out of the depths, gave me stability and is now one of the greatest joys in my life. Exercise is an absolute essential in our lives.

Go out and find what resonates with you.

Challenge: Consider the opportunities you have to exercise. Is there one you've always wanted to try, but never made the time for? Was there something you did as a child that got away from you? Pick one and set a time this week to do that activity for half-an-hour.

Chapter 12

Surfing

Too often do we distract ourselves inside our imaginations. We dwell on mistakes of the past. We worry about the future. We find ourselves transfixed and living in our heads. It's so easy to get caught up in these thoughts that our actual life passes us by.

Especially in my teens to early twenties, I imagined all the solutions to my problems lay elsewhere. Life in high school sucks, once I get to college things will get better. The people at this college aren't that great, once I transfer things will be better. America's culture has so many problems, once I'm abroad things will be better. On and on I lived with this approach. Where I was wasn't where I was meant to be. I believed my utopia lay elsewhere and once I arrived, I would finally be at peace.

At some point I became fixated on the idea of surfing. I would daydream constantly about how great it would be to paddle out onto the ocean every day. How relaxing and at ease I would be. There I would find community and fulfillment. Clearly, I was never content because I never lived near the ocean. That's what was missing. I finally figured it out. I knew that's where was meant to be. I was absolutely certain.

The classic idiom, "the grass is always greener on the other side" dominated my life.

I would say there are many angles to this, many things to be cautious of and consider. First, if you have dreams of exploring and traveling, absolutely go do it. Especially when you are young and not burdened with commitments or too many responsibilities, travel. There are so many benefits to traveling and expanding your world view. Both good and bad.

You get to see what the world is really like. It's quite a visceral experience to actually physically go explore areas you've only seen in movies, tv or through photos or the internet. Seeing how other people live, seeing what life is like changes you in the best ways.

It also shows you the reality. The truth of the world is that there are no perfect places. Nowhere is everyone happy and the people all get along and everything is perfect. There is no paradise without drawbacks here on Earth. Everywhere someone is sick of it, someone's depressed, someone's trying to escape. Your dream fantasy may be someone else's prison.

You may find that by traveling you find somewhere that better suits you and I certainly hope you do. I found that my interests and passions in life are heavily intertwined with mountains and the outdoors. In that regard, my birthplace of Minnesota didn't suit me, but to others it's a home they would never want to leave. Both choices are perfectly acceptable.

My caution is to not be obsessed with your fantasies of the ideal future. What I mean is you will find a lot more joy and fulfillment by focusing on what you have now.

For me living in Colorado I was blessed to be in what I consider one the greatest states in the United States. The scenery is beyond spectacular, the weather is great year-round, and the people are friendly. There is snowboarding, rock-climbing, an incredible music scene, hiking, camping, really a seemingly endless range of ways to stay engaged and active. With all these limitless things to do, I was obsessed with the one thing you can't do in Colorado. Surf.

So, if you were in my circumstances, you could spend every day daydreaming about the ocean and how good it would be to surf and think how limited Colorado is in that regard. Or you could keep your dreams of the ocean for the future and focus on what you have now. Is the glass half empty, is it half full? Your perspective is everything.

If you are in this thought loop, you will likely be empty wherever you go. When you get to the ocean you may miss the mountains. Or maybe it'll be too expensive, or the people aren't as nice, the city isn't as great. Constantly using some external stimuli as an excuse for your lack of fulfillment.

One of the greatest things you can do for yourself is learn how to be truly content with less. Be truly happy that. Although you long for the ocean, you are in the prairies of cornfields and that's ok too. There's beauty everywhere.

We love to rank and categorize items of our lives. This is better than that. Surfing is more fun than snowboarding. Mountains are better than oceans. Cities have more than small towns. The more you become engaged the more you will find that things are simply different, not better, not worse. Say what is better a ski trip to Aspen or a beach trip to Cancun? These experiences are too different to really compare. Learn to love where you are, what you have now, and your life will be much more fulfilling.

The other option is to never be fulfilled, never be satisfied and to constantly be chasing something that will never come. Be present, all there will ever be is here and now.

Challenge: Take an inventory of your thoughts. Are you daydreaming about an idyllic future? Is it somewhere you want to travel, a job you want, a partner you wish you had? Now shift your focus to your current circumstances. Take a moment to think of your current opportunities, the people and places in your day-to-day life. Make a list of things you are currently grateful for. Make a note of opportunities that are available you could take advantage of.

Chapter 13

Plateaus

I want to forewarn you about an obstacle that will arise along your journey. Especially as you stay consistent with your new habits and mental paradigms you will find yourself reaching plateaus. In recovery groups this point is often described as leaving the "pink cloud."

For those unfamiliar, the pink cloud is a state of perception one may feel as they are on the road of recovery. There are multiple ways one may experience the pink cloud and I will give you a few examples.

One instance is the pink cloud an alcoholic may feel after they quit drinking. They may notice they go to sleep earlier, have more energy, their stomach is more settled, their mind is clearer and have an overall happier disposition. These feelings can charge that individual with hope that they are on the right path and that the changes they have made are worthwhile.

Someone who starts exercising for the first time may notice similar feelings. Eating healthier, meditating daily, journaling, etc. All of these and countless other examples initially can create a euphoric state of being.

Unfortunately, this state is not permanent. Over time these blissful feelings may begin to fade and people enter a new state of "normal." Suddenly it's a little harder to get out of bed, meditation no longer brings this ultimate state of clarity, the rush from going to the gym has warn off. Not that these habits do nothing, it's just the feelings may be less intense.

The danger in leaving the pink cloud is that for many they will go back to their old ways. Go back to drinking, quit going to the gym, quit eating right, etc. Sometimes this will even go on in a loop. For years I was stuck in a loop where I would binge drink, go totally sober for months, feel better, feel worse and then go back to drinking. This is not the way to lasting success.

I think of these plateaus as reaching new levels. For the gamers out there, I hope this metaphor lands with you and those that aren't I will elaborate. What happens is that you are in one stage of life, imagining your ideal, who you'd like to be, the habits you'd like to have, the goals you want to accomplish. What will happen is that you reach these benchmarks and then you have a "now what" sensation.

At first your goal may be to lose fifty pounds. You hit the gym, get your diet in order and after months of work you finally do it. Now what? Maybe you want to stay here. Maybe your goal is to just be someone that works out a few times a week and maintains their body. Maybe you decide you want to train for a marathon.

Say you've never left your home state and it's always been a dream of yours to travel. You take a week off work and go on a road-trip around the country. Then you go on a longer trip. Then you fly to Europe. Next year you go to Asia. After a few years you've been around the globe, you're a seasoned traveler, now what are your goals? Do you simply want to see new places, do you want to interact with cultures more deeply, do you want to have your career intertwine with your travels?

As you reach your goals you change and as such your goals will evolve too. There's a scaling that happens. First you want to get out of debt, then you want to live comfortably, then you want to have true financial freedom. This is great. It's great to keep pushing your boundaries and reaching further.

The lesson I want to impart is that when you master your new habits, new ways of thinking, you will reach a new normal. You may not notice the effects perceptually anymore, but they are still working. Believe me if you stop doing them you will notice.

Let's take the example of tidying your living space. If you have lived somewhere clean and organized for months or years, you will have had the benefit of less clutter in your mental space. You will become accustomed to this. If you start to ignore your daily maintenance and let things fall into disarray your mind will follow too. With habits like these there will likely be a limit to the maximum return on investment so to speak. There's a barrier to how far cleaning will improve your overall wellbeing.

Know however that there are no limits on how far you can improve yourself. You can always use your time more efficiently, learn more, give more and be more. Don't think that means you have to chase some never-ending desire to be the best. That's another trap. Just know that as you reach new heights, those heights will become your normal and then you'll have to dream even higher. That's why the journey is so much more important than the destination, it never ends.

Chapter 14

Failure

What a daunting concept failure is. So much weight can be felt simply in the word. There is a commonly held idea that without success we are somehow doomed to a meaningless existence. It can be hard to articulate, often it's more of a gut feeling, a deep pit in our stomach that terrifies us. Many, many, many years I feared failing. I held the belief that if I failed at my pursuits my life would be wasted. I doubted my abilities so much that nearly any dream that held value to me I abandoned. Lack of experience, lack of connections, or simply an innate idea that I wasn't worthy made me quit. Hundreds if not thousands of times, I quit.

As a child I dreamed of being a game designer. Then when ideas of success infected my mind, how few people actually make it into that world, how difficult it is, I quit. In college film captured me. I transferred to a film school. After two semesters of learning about the industry the same fears arose. My lack of connections, the unlikelihood of being discovered, the competitive nature of the industry, I rationalized my fears as practicality and abandoned my dreams. Not just career paths. Relationships I didn't pursue because of feelings of inadequacy. Projects I procrastinated. All stemming from the same source: a fear of failure.

In my experience this feeling is universal. I have never met a single human being that at one point did not have to overcome this hurdle. I guarantee whoever your icons are no matter their success, their confidence, they had to cross this barrier too. Throughout this chapter I will share with you a few ideas to help you overcome this obstacle. First, you need to know that failing will actually be one of your greatest allies.

You will have many teachers in your life, friends that lift you up and opponents that try to tear you down. You might wish for a world that was all love and support, but the truth is resistance strengthens us. Failure lies somewhere in the middle-ground of these modalities. We learn by making mistakes. We try something, it doesn't work out, we see our error and try again.

Next you need to know failing is not the end. It is nothing to be feared or avoided, in fact the opposite is the case. Failure is necessary, failure will lead to you to liberation and freedom, failure is one of your greatest allies.

What do you mean failure is my friend?

Let me repeat **FAILURE IS YOUR FRIEND.**

Anyone who has ever attempted anything worthwhile and has achieved success, first encountered failure. No one was born a prodigy, no one was gifted with innate talent. "Success" has only every been achieved by breaking through and overcoming failure.

But so and so was naturally gifted, xyz picked it up right away, what about them? While it is true there are outliers who may be more naturally inclined toward certain disciplines, their minds better suited, their bodies better fit, they still have to put in work.

Look at someone like Michael Phelps. 28-time Olympic medalist. Michael Phelps was born 6' 4" with a wingspan over six feet. His body seems destined to be in the water. There is a mindset that would like to say his success is due to his genetic gifts. While there is an element of truth in that, it is mostly false. He was still the one to get up each morning and practice. He fed himself. He swam those events. His accomplishments are his creation. Beyond that if you are living under the mindset that our success is due to the genetic lottery, you're dooming yourself to a passive existence. Your whole life then is just a by-product of cause and effect. Determinism that you're fated for success or failure. The true masters exist because they have worked the long hours and put in the effort into their craft that they reached the state of mastery.

See failure as the first step necessary towards success. Think of it as paying your dues if that suits you. Know that every failure is just bringing you one step closer towards success. After each attempt you grow, you become a little wiser, a little more attune, one step closer to the person you are aiming to be. Step by step, inch by inch, you slowly progress until one day you are there.

People are often afraid to fail because of embarrassment. What will others think of me if I fail? What will I do if everyone sees me fail? Better to stay in the shadows to avoid that embarrassment.

One thing that may sound cold, but will help keep your ego in check, is to know that no one cares about what you're doing. Your parents and loved ones may wish you all the best, but they will never be as invested in your success as you will. More importantly strangers won't think of you the second you're out of their sight.

Say you're an aspiring musician and you decide to prop up on a street corner to perform. You're a little clunky, people stare at you odd, maybe even laugh, but they will never remember you. You are a long-forgotten memory in their eyes. Yet so much of our anxiety and angst is over their opinions. Let me tell you that anyone that would mock you is so terrified of doing what you're doing and that's why they cope. A "professional" musician would likely see you be impressed at your courage and tell you to keep going. Whose opinion do you hold in higher esteem, the strangers that are too afraid to try or the pro who was in your spot years ago?

The best example I think to help illustrate this is giving a speech in front of a classroom. Whether in High School or University, at some point almost everyone has had to give a speech or presentation in front of their peers. How daunting this can be. Many people have come to the consensus that public speaking is the greatest of all fears. More so than death. People would rather drop dead than have to speak in front of others. Let that sink in for a moment... Seriously, given the option of death or talking for five min in front of others, people would often choose the former... Wow.

I won't pretend like I never was afraid speaking in front of others or that I don't still get the jitters sometimes. For me, I spoke to my classmates, I did door-to-door sales and I now teach yoga. Now most of the time I really think nothing of speaking in front of others. Why? Because no one cares, no one is noticing all your mistakes.

How do I know this? Because in any of my speech classes when others were going, I noticed I didn't care. Usually I was thinking about how their speech compared to mine. Did they have more material then me? I thought about what I would say when it was my turn to present. I would certainly notice someone who was shaky, or nervous. I was aware of it, but this was no concern was it of mine.

Such a simple example, but I hope you realize how far this extends in life. I have met so many people who are unfathomably nervous about going to the gym. Their nervousness stems from fear.

Usually, not always, the example I most often hear is that someone is overweight and they are afraid of being seen in the gym, judged and ridiculed. Most of the time, no one notices you at the gym. When I'm at the gym there are basically two people that catch my attention. One is someone who is on the machine I want to use and I'm trying to gauge when they'll leave. The other is the loud, obnoxious, using three machines and six sets of dumbbells type.

I will add that unfortunately there is sometimes reasons for this fear. There are bullies. People who are cruel and whose self-esteems are so small that the only way they can feel powerful is to put down others and this can happen at the gym. These people are an absolute poison for the world. You should not allow their toxic behavior to shape your life.

You could be overweight, absolutely jacked, tall, short, skinny, etc. it doesn't matter. Whatever your disposition, I have nothing, but the utmost respect for people that make taking care of their body as a priority. Those that are overweight in the gym to me are an absolute source of inspiration.

I think it takes a tremendous amount of courage and self-awareness to try and improve yourself. It is no small feet and it really warms my heart to see people putting in real effort to change their circumstances.

I will say that continuing to pursue a goal there is no failure. You ran the race and got in second, you asked that person out and they said no, you applied for the job and were rejected. Those are not failures. Those are stepping-stones on your journey to success, each one bringing you a little closer.

There is only one true failure. Quitting is failure. I say that with the largest possible asterisk I can. Sometimes goals are no longer worth pursuing. Sometimes you need to let things go, but if it's something you want, that you still believe in, and you quit, that is failure.

I won't lie or pretend to you that it is easy to know when that is either. How do you know when it is time to throw in the towel? When have you given it enough? That's for you to decide.

Some of my favorite people in this world are stand-up comedians. For many reasons, but one in particular Bill Burr has always stood out to me for his work ethic. Someone had asked him about his journey, how long it took to catch his break and he described his career this way.

Bill said he worked for ten years without really any success. Living on friend's couches, not getting very good responses from crowds, just sort of getting by for ten years. Working college campuses, comedy clubs, restaurants, wherever he could find work. Eventually success came. He became an established name, released specials, became a television and movie star. Now he has the freedom to do whatever he pleases. I have such awe and reverence for that sort of perseverance. Truly when I think about that I'm mind blown.

I think it poses a really interesting question of what do you want in life? What would you be willing to work ten years for without a sign of success and keep going? When you enjoy your craft, simply just by doing it you are a success. Bill might not have been successful in a material monetary way for years, but he found true success pursuing his passion and calling. One interesting insight came from a career orientated friend of his that had all the traditional staples of success. Wealth, big home, established family. Bill described a time when this friend listened to him perform and wished they had something in their life that made them feel the way stand-up made Bill feel. All that wealth and symbols of success brought them nothing.

When you let go of when things come to be you will find peace. If you don't care how long it takes, you will reach the end. It will happen. Sit down, do the work and it will happen.

Let go of how it comes to be and just get to work.

"Failures"

Before moving on to the next section I wanted to share a few examples of some "failures" throughout history. These individuals persevered through rejection, loss, and a myriad of other circumstances. May their journeys inspire and give you the conviction to persevere on your own.

Thomas Edison

Credited for inventing the lightbulb, Thomas Edison's career had a start that would surprise most. From an early age his teachers said he was a "too stupid to learn anything," "asked too man questions" and eventually would be homeschooled where he learned by teaching himself to read and performing experiments in the basement. He was fired from two jobs for being "non-productive" and held over 1,000 patents for the lightbulb that never worked.

Over one thousand times Thomas Edison tried and failed to get the lightbulb to come on. He eventually succeeded and much of the way the modern world operates is due to his perseverance. When asked how he felt about failing a thousand times he replied.

"I didn't fail 1,000 times. The lightbulb was an invention with 1,000 steps."

Walt Disney

Famous creator was originally fired as a newspaper editor because, "he lacked imagination and had no good ideas." This would only be the start of his journey. The first animation studio he attempted quickly went bankrupt in 1921. At one point he was subsiding off dog food simply to survive.

He would restart several more times before going on to create one of the most successful and influential companies in the world. Beyond a simple animation studio with amusement parks, The Walt Disney Company now spans multiple industries and is worth hundreds of billions.

Michael Jordan

No doubt one of the greatest basketball players of all time, Michael Jordan like all the others listed here overcame many hurdles to reach his dreams. As a teenager, he tried out for his varsity team and was cut for not being tall enough or good enough. Rather than quit and give up, Michael persevered through the naysayers and went on to be one of the greatest in his field. Together MJ and his team won six NBA Championships.

"I have missed more than 9,000 shots in my career. I have lost almost 300 games. On 26 occasions I have been entrusted to take the game winning shot, and I missed. I have failed over and over and over again in my life. And this is why I succeed."

Michael was no stranger to failure and used it to fuel his own journey.

"If you're trying to achieve, there will be roadblocks. I've had them; everybody has had them. But obstacles don't have to stop you. If you run into a wall, don't turn around and give up. Figure out how to climb it, go through it, or work around it."

Chapter 15

Success

What is success? There is some vague notion of what it means to be successful. There are ideas culturally we are raised on that influence are perception of what it means. Different cultures around the world vary as to what it is specifically, but everywhere we are all chasing success.

Often, we can't quite articulate what it is specifically. We judge others. We sort ourselves into a hierarchy and define success that way. The man in the suit with the nice car, big house, prestigious job at the esteemed company, he's a success right? The woman with the perfectly fitted outfit, the work life balance, perfect children, the dream Instagram account, she's a success right? We're led to believe these markers are indicators of success.

More importantly, we are led to believe without these things we are incomplete.

Athletes, musicians, actors, those who are at the peak of their fields that must be success. Those who won the awards, who have the most subscribers, sold the most books, have the most followers, they're successful.

Right?

There are milestones you can ascribe to define success. Checkmarks of things accomplished. Graduated high school, graduated college, a career, a family, retirement plan... These are ideas that collectively we have decided are what it means to have made it.

What you will find in life is that it all depends. I'm not going to tell you that achieving these moments or other goals you have is success or isn't. Some truly want the "traditional" life, want a nice home, a steady career and a family to come home to. To many that is success, to others it's a prison.

Some are driven to endure the long nights, the many years and the countless hours spent in medical school to become doctors. Others, are on that path because of what was expected of them or pressured on them by their family or society.

Many will see someone living out of their van as an absolute failure, an underachiever, a hippy burnout. To others van-dwelling is the ultimate form of freedom. A life unconstrained by the limits of leases or mortgages. It's up to each person to define their own identity for what it means to be successful. Note too that just as our we grow and change, so to do our dreams and aspirations. What we want and value changes over time. Allowing room for our goals to evolve is just as important as staying resolute and dedicated to our mission.

As you start conceptualizing your own ideal scenario of the person you want to be, the life you want to lead, a few bits of insight will help guide you along your path. The first being the downfall of comparison.

It's easy to get discouraged when we are comparing ourselves to others. You go to the gym, you are overweight and see the model human, six pack, tan, idealized god or goddess and you feel discouraged.

You pick up the guitar. When you start strumming some chords clumsily you can't help but notice those with more experience. Your friend hammers away with ease singing and dancing creating a wonderous melody.

Perhaps you paddle out onto the ocean on a surfboard. The waves crash against you. You spend all day just trying to simply stand up and are knocked down over and over. Meanwhile the locals glide across the waves with ease.

You must know a few things to keep you going along the path towards success.

Firstly, if you are attempting something you have no experience in whether that's fitness, a new job, a new hobby, dating, eating healthy, etc. you will not be good at first You will suck. Sure, there's a chance you may surprise yourself by picking up a hobby quickly, but don't count on it. Go in being fully be prepared to start from the absolute lowest point of whatever discipline you are undertaking.

From here, there's nowhere to go but up. You suck at the piano. Great. That's totally fine. Know you can only get better. If you practice and are persistent you will inevitably get better. Don't worry about the time. However long it takes is just fine. It will take as long as it needs to. Simply know, the more time you put into anything, the more consistently you keep up with it, the quicker you will get better at it.

Not many things in life offer guarantees. Absolute certainty is a rare commodity. Hopefully you can see the magic then that through persistence, improvement is guaranteed. Through repetition and persistence no goal is out of reach, it's simply a matter of time. The length of time is in direct proportion to your effort.

For instance, if you practice yoga once a week, you will slowly start noticing yourself become more flexible, the postures easier, and your body stronger. If you practice twice a week, you'll notice improvements quicker. Three times even more so. You get the idea.

Also, apply the same concept if you are neglecting your goals. If you aim to hit the gym five times a week, and then take a week off, and then only go twice a week, you'll likely notice a stagnation or decline in your abilities.

Sometimes life gets in the way. Work picks up, or your car breaks down, a relationship implodes, a loved one passes... sometimes there are unforeseen consequences that get in the way. Sometimes it's not practical to pursue our goals. If you dream of backpacking the Appalachian Trail, but you are in the middle of a two-year nursing school degree your dream will have to wait. That's ok. It's ok to have dreams and goals that are for another day.

What's important though is to make the most of the time you have now and to be using it in the most effective way possible. Think about it in terms of maximizing your time.

While I was in school, I thought about how I could best use my days. Typically, I would be in school for a few hours each day, with varying gaps of time in between. If I had a few hours free, that would be a good space to go to the gym. Give myself time to workout, get back have a meal, and recuperate before class. If I only had an hour or so between class, maybe I would read a book, meditate, or listen to a podcast.

Take an inventory of your own life. When do you have gaps? What is your schedule? I **HIGHLY** recommend making an excel sheet or use another app to actually map out your days and plan your goals that way. If you want to start working out, when are you going to do it? After work, before, on your lunch break? Make a time for it and stick to it. Or create spaces where you have options.

Realize that what you are undertaking as you begin or are along your path is that you are on a journey of growth. What's the cliché, it's not the destination it's the journey. Well clichés exist for a reason. I would say that both parts are necessary.

The destination gives you an endpoint. Something to shoot for and guide you along your path. The journey is where you will actually do the work, have the experiences, grow and become the person you wish to be.

Being too fixated on the end is a dangerous game that can actually dissuade or end your quest. Again, I'll return to the example of weight loss. If you are 100 pounds overweight and you want to lose that weight that's fantastic. It's a wonderful thing to attempt to make your body healthier.

It's also very difficult, takes a lot of time, commitment and dedication. Weight loss is different for everyone. Some people cutout soda, or beer, stop eating fast-food and shed 20 pounds seemingly overnight. Others spend multiple days at the gym, eat nothing, but healthy foods and lose a pound or less every week. It's not "fair" but we're all unique and are dealt different cards in life.

The secret to staying on the path and not being overcome with discouragement will be your attitude. Every day aim to be a little better. Every day you step foot in the gym is a step in the right direction. It is getting you one step closer to the person you want to be. Every time you take time to meditate is a victory.

It's so easy to compare ourself to others, but if you want to know the true victory, it's being better than the person you were the day before. It's subtle. You won't wake up and be a drastically different human being. But if you stick with your goals, day by day you will become the person you want to be.

Then when you look back on yourself months or years later you will be astounded by your progress. I went from an awkward gamer kid, who never exercised, never committed to goals, was always the victim of circumstances to who I am now. I'm a yoga teacher, I've traveled the world, I'm very outgoing, and every year I raise the bar and become someone a little bit more. I'm actually very satisfied with how my journey has panned out. To me the stories of rising from an absolute "loser" to someone you are proud of are much more interesting than someone who never overcame obstacles. Know the latter don't really exist, we all have obstacles to overcome. It's easy to assume from the outside that the successful people were born with it or just got there by fluke, or nepotism, or whatever other excuse. The truly successful had to earn their place and you will too.

Focus on your own path. Know that if you invest the time, stay committed and let go of how things come to be there is nothing you can't achieve.

Inevitable success. Think about how magical that is for a moment. There aren't many things in life that are inevitable. There's no guarantee you'll fall in love, no guarantee you'll be a millionaire, no guarantee you'll be famous. All of those things are pretty much out of your control. What is in your control is success though. You can pursue something for so long that you inevitably become a master at it, inevitably obtain success. If that's not motivating, I don't know what is.

Detach yourself from the outcome. Do not look at your goals in terms of winning or losing. By trying you have already won. It sounds counter intuitive, like how can there be no winners or losers. Well you lose by not trying. If you write a book and no one reads it, that's still infinitely more impressive than someone too scared of failure that never tried. If you go to an open mic night and are booed off stage, it's more impressive than someone too afraid to show up. Do it for yourself. What do you care what the audience thinks? Why do you put so much weight into the opinions of strangers? Live up to your own standards and ignore your critics and naysayers. It's easy to be a critic, everyone has an opinion. It takes a lot more courage to create something, to bring it forth into the world and stand by it because you believe it has merit.

Challenge: Think of a goal. Imagine your future self and what it would mean to be successful. Do you have the job you always dreamed of? Did you create that piece of art you've been fantasizing of? Is it a place you want to see, a skill you wish you had? What would make you think you are successful? Once you have this idea in mind work it backwards. What steps do you need to take to get there? Take the first step today.

Chapter 16

Mindset

This next chapter will outline different attitudes and mindset adjustments that will help guide you. Just as a carpenter has many tools to build a home, hammers for nails, saws to cut wood and plyers to pry. Each tool has a specific job and function. I want you to think of these topics as different tools in your mindset toolbox. They all serve different roles and will help you overcome unique obstacles. Play with each, learn when to use them and you will master one of the greatest opponents in life. The mind. Our thoughts often run amuck. They are driven by immediate gratification, poor learned habits and lack of clarity. Robin Sharma put it quite elegantly, "The mind is a wonderful servant, but a terrible master." Learn these concepts and you will become the master of your mind.

Contentment

Attitude is everything. The way you view your experiences is more important than the actual experiences themselves. There are those that have "everything", wealth, relationships, power, status, fame, every fantasy fulfilled and yet aren't satisfied. There are those that enough is never enough. No matter how good they have it, there will always be an imperfection something could be better. They are seemingly cursed with an insatiable appetite for more.

As they chase their goals, they may end up achieving them. In fact, they may excel and be quite successful. Yet each milestone and every achievement leads to a perpetual never ending cycle of want that will never cease. Then there is their counterpart.

Those that have "nothing" and yet have everything. There are people who work three jobs, never travel, are unknown to the public, and yet these people have found lasting fulfillment. They may yearn to improve their circumstances, while simultaneously being content with what is. That is the key.

For years I struggled and wrestled with this concept. Many Buddhists, new age philosophers, and others espouse being content in the present. To not wish to change or alter the present. Everything is already perfect as it is. They are correct. The present is perfect. Who you are, where you are, what you are is exactly what needs to be.

One of the most profound thoughts I have ever heard came from Paul Selig, who works as a conduit for voices he calls the guides. In one of his dictations he stated, "all is of or nothing is." Meaning that everything and every moment is divine in the highest sense, or nothing is. There is no hierarchy, no better no worse, everything is perfect. This is a concept intellectually I agree with, have had moments where I felt I understand, but even typing this now I still struggle with.

It is very difficult for me to really feel the painful, heartbreaking, annoying, rage inducing experiences of life as divine. I find it extraordinarily difficult to experience moments of anguish and moments of pure bliss and say they are of equal merit. They are, but as I present this idea to you, I want you to know I still struggle with it so if it sounds completely backwards, I don't blame you.

What I'm trying to impart with you, though, is that if you can be content in the "worst" of circumstances, you will have the power to overcome anything. We are often afraid to make certain choices out of fear of how we would handle it. People stay in jobs they don't like so they can afford to maintain their current lifestyles.

Say your dream was to be a standup comedian and for years you've worked as an HR rep. You have a nice place, health benefits, great salary, etc. Life is predictable, steady, yet not fulfilling. For years you've held this dream in your head. You want to go for it, but you're afraid what it will mean to commit to your dream.

If you don't have a steady source of income how will you afford your nice apartment? What would it mean to go back to living with roommates or couch surfing? How will you handle no longer being able to afford the high-end grocery store, or your custom espresso from the gourmet coffee shop? What will your family think when you've tossed away your secure safe structured job for some wild dream? What about all those years you spent in school, all those years you spent climbing the ladder? The list of fears and questions is endless. It can paralyze you into inaction or make you rationalize giving up entirely.

I was very blessed to have lived in quite varying degrees of living standards throughout my life. I grew up in a very modest home living off the basics. Then, later in life I was privileged to live in some quite nice places. Went to good schools. Lived in the heart of the city in a one bedroom. Lived in a "luxury" apartment right off campus. Couched surfed with friends and finally am writing this book from what can only be described as a closet with a bunkbed in a rural ski hamlet. Can't say

I lived in the worst of places. Fortunate to have never been homeless or somewhere exceptionally dangerous. I have lived a very large range of quite elegant to utterly basic. I will tell you that the experience overall is mostly the same.

Having a nice place is great, but unessential. At the end of the day I come home, sleep in a bed and it's mostly the same experience. When you're worried about potentially "downgrading" or how you'll cope, trust that you are strong and adaptable. People have an incredible tolerance for what they can handle. You will surprise yourself with how strong you are. Our earliest ancestors slept on barren earth, I think you'd find a couch or a van an easy alternative to that.

In order to improve our circumstances, we often have to sacrifice our immediate comforts for long-term gains. I promise this is always worth it. Choosing the opposite, immediate gratification at the cost of your long-term happiness never is. Those are choices made in fear that will lead to regret.

Fear will be something you will have to contend with in many avenues of life. I hope that one day you will see it as your ally in a way. For I believe that a big part of our journeys is overcoming our fears. We all have fears. Some things that are terrifying to some are a joke to others. It's not about what others are dealing with though it's your own. To quote Greg Plitt, "On the other side of fear is the person you want to be." Truly when you conquer your fears you rise to the next level. You become that person you have always dreamed of and see with such clarity. It is like climbing to the peak of a mountain and finally being able to see the vista around you. 360 degrees of clarity. That is conquering your fears.

There are a few tools I can give you that will ease the grip fear has over you. One is to know that fear may never go away and that everyone is fearful. Often times we look to our heroes who appear fearless. They do what they want despite criticism and those who wish to tear them down.

It's not that they don't feel fear, it's that they do the things they need to do regardless of their fears.

Feast or Famine

Another idea for your mindset toolbox is what I like to describe as the feast or feminine attitude. Plenty or limited resources. One thought loop that is easy to be trapped by is the notion of there not being enough. That the person who broke your heart was the only one and now you are doomed to be alone forever. That dream job you had for the dream company rejected you and now you will be unfulfilled. You were denied from your perfect school and now you'll never have the career you want.

On and on this goes and can be applied. I will tell you now that we live in a world of plenty. As of writing this book there are 7.8 billion people on this planet. So if you're worried about finding love, know that you could be the most unlikable human being ever, say one percent of all the people you meet enjoy your company. That's 78 million people. Plenty of fish in the sea doesn't even come close to explaining that.

You're worried about not getting some job because you didn't go to some school or whatever other excuse you have in your mind. There are so many stories of people who had nothing, absolutely nothing, circumstances so much worse than yours and rose to such heights. There is an abundance of opportunities in this world. Align yourself on the side of plenty.

Awareness

Here is where your mind is not always your ally. In this specific instance is where your mind is actually working the hardest against you. To start, you have to understand that your mind's main objective is to achieve homeostasis. To keep things in the status quo. This can be beneficial, however if you have bad habits, negative thought patterns or other undesirable circumstances your mind will actually work to keep these going.

It hates change. Change to the mind is dangerous. It is actually functioning on a purely instinctual biological level. This may have served us during the time of hunter-gatherers, but not so much in this day and age. For example, in my overused favorite analogy of exercising, your mind will see this as a danger if it's not part of your normal routine.

Beyond muscles being atrophied or not used to working out, mentally your brain sees this increase and heartrate, depletion of energy as a danger. Something must be wrong shut this down immediately.

When you are working out or doing something outside your comfort zone, your mind is going to tell you to stop. "Don't talk to strangers, why would you do that, we never do that, just go home." "Why are you eating these green foods, these aren't as salty or flavorful as that greasy burger." "Why are we waking up so early I'm tired go back to bed." There is this voice in your head that for a long while you will have to contend with and actively fight.

Back to exercising. You will notice two situations when you are working out. One is that you reach your physical limit. You push as hard as you can possibly go and there is nothing left. You collapse to the ground, your arms give out, you're done. If you are doing this safely congratulations because that is a hard place to reach and you should be commended for it. The other place you will notice, maybe more often than not is your mind telling you you've reached your limit.

Just a couple days ago, I was backcountry snowboarding with a friend of mine. As we were climbing to the top, I was bombarded with all of these negative thoughts. "I need a break, I have to catch my breath, we've been going for hours I need a moment to collect myself, I need water now!" These thoughts were doing circles in my mind edging me into stopping, quitting, and giving up. One trick I've learned to help bring my awareness back into my body is taking deep breaths.

In through the nose, out through the mouth. After a few of these I was able to pause and bring awareness back into my body. Was I really out of breath? No, I was breathing hard a while ago, but actually I feel pretty calm. Are my legs too tired to keep going? No, honestly they felt just fine. Was I dehydrated? No actually, took I tiny sip of water and felt perfectly fine.

Physically, I was working, but nowhere near my limit. My mind wanting to maintain status quo, though, and was not stoked to be climbing up that mountain. Your challenges may not be in the mountains and may not even be physical. I can tell you that so much of my social anxieties I used this same method and found tremendous relief.

Even something as simple as eating a meal. We've all had the instance where we feel like we're absolutely starving. We order or prepare a banquet for ourselves. In our intoxicated state of hunger, we gorge ourselves. Then at the end our stomachs are cramped and we feel as if we are about to burst. Rather than shovel food into your mouth as quickly as you can when you eat, relax and take your time. Notice how you feel. Are you filling up, do you really need more, do you really want desert? So often we act on autopilot on our instincts

It's always a good idea to bring your awareness back into yourself. Take a deep breath. Scan your whole body. Head to toes. Notice are you holding tension. Are you really as tired as your mind says you are? Take inventory of your internal state. Become aware of yourself.

Victim Mindset

One of the biggest pitfalls that will keep you stuck is the victim mindset. What I mean by this is believing that your circumstances, your life, your problems were put on you by someone else. This will be a challenge for many and even as you hone this skill, you will have to keep this in check.

Playing the victim card is an easy way to opt out of taking responsibility of our lives. It's easy to say that I'm messed up because of how my parents raised me. I'm overweight because I grew up on fast food. I'm in debt because society won't give me a break. I can't trust people because my significant other cheated on me. I'm not telling you that people haven't wronged you, that society isn't unfairly balanced, or that how you were raised hasn't impacted who you are now.

By claiming and identifying with this mindset you are doing yourself a tremendous disservice and the next step for your growth is to free yourself from it. When any of these victim thoughts come to mind my favorite response to them is "yes, and what are you going to do about it?"

Say as you were growing up your parents whether they didn't know it wasn't good for you or it was all they could afford fed you nothing, but high octane, sugar ridden, fast food. Years and years went by reinforcing your addiction and as long as you have known that's all you ate. One day in your mid-thirties you look in the mirror and think how unfair it was. They fed you, they did this to you, you want to be fit, but your parents made you this way... Yes, and what are you going to do about it?

At some point you have to claim your life as your own. Yes, when you are a child, you are pretty much at the mercy of your parent's judgements and choices. As regular people, they undoubtedly make mistakes. They likely didn't try to, maybe they didn't know, maybe they were overworked, maybe any number of reasons, but as people they tried their best and came up short in some moments. In this instance, they did not imprint on you the need for a nutritious diet and unfortunately fed the flames of an addiction to food that doesn't serve you.

Regardless, at some point you also chose to keep going. Somewhere along the line you learned what foods were good and bad. You knew that going for those sweets wasn't what you needed, but it's what you wanted. You made those choices. We choose to stay addicted. We choose to stay stuck.

We are often conflicted in these moments. Like a smoker who knows it's not good for them, but caves into their desires. Use whatever metaphor or analogy you like, but we always decide. The victim mindset allows the ego to stay soothed. It tells you that you didn't decide to be this way, it was so-and-sos fault. You didn't have any say and you never will. This is a lie.

You always have a choice. I'm not telling you it will be easy. Especially with addictions, old thought patterns, bad habits, cycles can be extremely hard to break. It is essential though and when you break through these obstacles you will be the person you've always dream of.

What I will tell you is that you are stronger than any adversity you have ever faced. If you are sitting here today reading this book or listening to it on a recording, you are stronger than your greatest challenges. Obviously, they didn't kill you, you're still here and you have the power to overcome anything that comes in your way.

Negative Self Talk

Be cautious of the words you use. They can elevate you to greatness or cripple your abilities. The words we use say a lot about how feel, how we perceive ourselves, and our sense of self-worth. These can be very subtle, but their influence is profound.

Most likely, the harshest critic you will have to deal with on your journey is yourself. We are unfairly hypercritical and unreasonable with our own personal expectations. Some of this is due to our conditioning. We are constantly bombarded with images and slogans purveying the message of living our "best" life. Are we as fit as we can be, are we as best-dressed as we can be, do we use our time in the most productive manner, are we maximizing our happiness?

There is a fine line here as these ideas in many ways are great. It's wonderful to use your time effectively. It's great to want to get the most out of your experience. Raising the bar on your own standards and becoming a better person is a noble aspiration. There would be no reason to read this book if you didn't aspire for something greater.

The problem lies in that medicine becoming a poison. As you move on your journey some days your progress will make leaps and bounds. Other times you may find yourself stagnating or even appearing to move backwards. It's easy for that voice in your head to turn sour.

"See you didn't have it in you, nothing will ever change, things are worse than before, what's the point you'll never reach it..."

It is important to be aware of the way we talk about ourselves. Say you're in the store picking up groceries and you spot a candy bar the grabs your eye. You buy it knowing in the back of your head that you don't need it and it's going to get in the way of your goals. If someone you know sees you, you may drop the excuse, "oh I just couldn't control myself..."

Notice in this situation how you see yourself. Really reflect on it. Are you so weak willed that by merely seeing a candy bar you lose all control and dive straight into your primal instincts? It doesn't have to be food. Say you want to give up drinking. Then you're watching a movie and the hero pours a nice tall glass of whiskey, lets out a satisfying, "ahhhh." You pull into the liquor store, grab yourself a bottle and live out the fantasy. Is that all it takes? You saw something on TV and now you lose sight of your goals and who you want to be.

"I couldn't control **myself**."

Notice the choice of words here. Here you are distinguishing I and myself as two distinct identities. Two separate forces. There are countless books, philosophers and others who have explored the differences between your ego and your true self. In this instance these are the two players I feel are in the game.

I is the real you. The true self that knows who it is, who it wants to be, what it has to do and so forth. Myself is the ego. Myself is the animalistic, primal, short-sighted shadow that you need to tame. Tame, not remove.

There is a shadow self that is a part of all of us that cannot be removed. You can remove poisons from your life: smoking, gambling, fast foods, etc. but you can't remove the desire, the wants, the cravings. It is a part of you and sorry to burst your bubble, but it always will be. This is not a bad thing. Your ego like everything else, when harnessed properly can very much be a tool for you to use to your advantage.

You must tame it first and one of the ways we do this is through our use of language. Let's go back to the grocery store. Your ego is in your head telling you how sweet that candy bar will be, how it won't hurt you, how you can go back to eating healthy, you've earned it. It will whisper sweet nothings into your ear trying to erode your will and get you to cave. These moments are crucial and one of the areas you can begin the most effective change.

It takes no effort in the sense of physical effort. No driving to get the food or ordering on an app. No extra effort. It's in these moments you need to hear this voice and say, "I hear you, but I am in charge and we're not having this candy bar today." Like a child who didn't get the toy it wants it may throw a temper tantrum in your head. It may whine and scream about how unfair you are and how stupid it is you didn't get the candy bar. On and on. Like a stern parent, you need to be stoic. You need to be unmoved by the angry child and stand your ground.

The more you do this, the more you will build your own voice and be able to stand by what you say. Your voice will carry weight and your choices will be made by your own volition. When you've really earned it and when it really serves you to indulge in the pleasures of life, by eating that candy bar or whatever the craving may be, you will be able to make that choice for yourself.

That's when life gets really interesting: when we live with intentions. When we see the big picture and look beyond the circumstances of our present. That is where the magic happens.

Change

Change is the nature of the universe. This is likely not the first time you've heard this but let me extrapolate this idea further. One danger that traps many of us is trying to make things last forever. Whether it's a relationship with a significant other, a night out in the city, or just a period in life where everything is in synch. We are blessed to have these moments of euphoria where things are exactly the way we've dreamed of and wouldn't it be great if they lasted forever.

Out of fear, we often will try to take steps to make sure to keep things from changing. If we're afraid of losing a partner maybe we get clingier, start texting nonstop, start questioning where our partner is going, who will be there. We feel so afraid that they'll leave and do everything we can to make sure they stay. How ironic that so many of these actions often push that person away. Actions based in fear tend to lead to that fear manifesting.

The film series Star Wars illustrated this beautifully in Revenge of the Sith. Anakin, the protagonist, is having visions of losing his wife Padme. He consults master Yoda about these dreams. Yoda offers some profound insight, "train yourself to let go of all that you are afraid to lose."

Anakin ultimately rejects this teaching and gives into the promises of the Dark side. When Padme sees what becomes of him, she eventually dies of a broken heart. He created the reality he so desperately wanted to avoid.

Especially with death, there is a tendency to look at it as a great tragedy. I can't answer for you the mysteries of what happens when we die. Is there an afterlife, do we die and that's it, are we reincarnated? No one knows, and I don't think anyone will ever know with absolute certainty. I can tell you with absolute certainty we will all die.

Everything ends and that's ok. Another film that highlighted this beautifully was in Troy where Achilles states, "The gods envy us because we're mortal, because any moment may be our last. Everything is more beautiful because we're doomed. You will never be lovelier than you are now. We will never be here again."

Treasure what you have because you had it, not because of its longevity. I've had friendships that lasted weeks or even days that were more meaningful and impactful then ones that lasted years. Relationships that spanned days that were more beautiful and fulfilling than ones going over months.

You can still mourn those that pass, be sad when a relationship ends, and be upset when something you treasured is broken. I'm not telling you not to feel, it's part of being human. All I'm saying that as you come to understand the impermanence of everything, your unhealthy attachment to things will diminish. As always there is a fine balance here. Not so unattached that you feel nothing, but not so attached that you are crippled when it's gone. You will find the space in between.

Sinking Ship

As you embark on your journey towards self-realization you may have the instinct to "save" others along the way. You may see others struggling with your same hardships. Perhaps this is a family member, a partner or a friend. Your compassionate heart may yearn to reach out and save them. While I applaud your selfless instinct, I caution you to have restraint with your actions.

It's not that you shouldn't help others, but when you are beginning your journey or in the early stages of it, often it is better to direct your efforts on your own path. In the event of a decompression on a plane, airliners will advise you to put your own air mask on before assisting your loved ones. This advice should guide you along your path towards self-improvement.

Another analogy that may be useful is a drowning person. Sadly, there are instances where someone is drowning and another swims out to save them. In their panic and confusion, the person drowning pulls them both under. This wasn't their intention, but it can happen all the same.

Say you're a smoker, your friends are smokers and you all decide to make a pact to quit together. You will be your own accountability buddies. Right off the start everything is great. Then after a week or so your friend had a long day at work, their kid ran a bicycle into their car, and exacerbated your friend went back to smoking. They caved under the pressure and now you're wondering whether or not you should keep going.

Perhaps when you've mastered your new goal you can help your loved ones. When you've gained the self-confidence and the where-with-all to endure the trials you can help them. Whatever obstacle you are facing will take effort. Make no mistake of that.

Some people seem to have no limits to what they can accomplish, but we all have our breaking points. Really combating your deepest challenges will take everything you have. As a result, you don't want to be expending your energy on someone else's path. Especially at the onset.

Crabs In A Bucket

Another one of my favorite analogies within this realm is the idea of crabs in a bucket. What comes as a shock to many is that when you begin improving your life, not everyone will be in support. Some will even actively work to discourage you and get you to quit.

The metaphor is saying there is a bucket of crabs in a restaurant. All waiting their turn on the chopping block. Some may try and escape this prison. As they do so, the crabs underneath will pull them back in. Misery loves company shares the same message.

Why is that the case? Why wouldn't people be happy for you? Why would they actively try to diminish or stop you? The reason is usually tied to a preservation of ego and dealing with insecurity. When you try and escape, or improve your circumstances, you actively trigger in their mind the knowledge that they aren't.

By reaching and striving for more, you unintentionally shine a light on their own failures. They know they aren't doing the work they need and rather than deal with that, they try to pull you down with them. Be mindful of those in your life that don't show support when you start improving. They may have snide comments, they may actively discourage you. Be wary of their intent and energy.

Be Selfish

I imagine that headline likely brought some shock or unpleasant feelings up amongst a few of you. One way no one wants to be labeled as is selfish. Selfish brings about many negative ideas. Self-centeredness, apathy and indifference towards others, and a belief that it all revolves around you. With everything there is a positive and negative side to being selfish. Since the ways I just highlighted are likely familiar to most I want to spend a little time to present the idea that being selfish can actually be the best thing you can do for yourself and the world at large.

In the modern world we are all inundated with crises that span the globe. From environmental disasters, terrorist attacks, collapsing economies and disease epidemics, it can often seem that everything is falling apart. As such, there is an attitude we have been presented that if you are not up to date and have a passionate stance on these issues you are selfish. You are self-centered, you don't care. This idea is nothing, but toxic and serves no one.

While there is value in being informed and aware of the problems that face our species, often the way we can truly best serve is by focusing our attention inwards. We all have problems in our lives, whether that's our own self-imposed limitations, bad habits, unfortunate circumstances, there are issues we must all face. Turning our focus on these issues allows us to not only become the best versions of ourselves, but also makes us better suited to serve our communities.

Think of a time you were really exhausted. Your boss kept you late at work all week, you hadn't been eating well, sleep deprived and unhappy, how did you behave as a member of the community? Did you immediately react with anger when someone cut you off on the highway? Were you annoyed when someone was moving slowly through the checkout line? Did you snap at your kids, your partner, your friends when they did something that slightly bugged you? These have been a lot of negative scenarios, let's look at the instances from another angle.

Take all these situations, but now let's see how you face them when things are going well. Say you met someone recently and the sparks are really flying in your relationship. Your boss has been extra kind to you and you even got an extra day off work this week. The weather is perfect and everything seems to be going right. Now someone cuts you off in traffic and you think, "it's ok I'm in no rush." Someone is taking forever to pay in the grocery line, but you don't have anywhere to be. Kids spilled milk on the floor, but you grab a towel and clean in up, no problem. The point I'm trying to illustrate is your overall state of being impacts the way you behave and interact with the world.

Why I am telling you it's ok to be "selfish" is that by focusing on yourself, your problems, you are actually serving everyone in the best way possible. For the true altruists who want nothing than to better mankind, this is actually the way. We are often led to believe that the only way to serve is by being martyrs and to sacrifice ourselves. There are instances where that is the case, but it does not always have to be this way. Things are never as black and white as that and the idea that is not discussed as often is the one I am trying to convey to you now.

One of the reasons I feel so inclined to speak so vehemently on this issue is that critics and others may actively try to stop you from bettering yourself. If you have a toxic partner that thrives on your attention and you start working on yourself, they may accuse you of being selfish. That going to the gym or focusing on your hobbies is somehow a bad thing. Your parents may do this, siblings, friends, people you trust as your allies may surprise you in their lack of support. Beyond not supporting you, they may actually discourage or try stopping you. Crabs in a bucket.

Your critics may attack you with the guise that you are selfish and that focusing your intentions inward is wrong. Clearly there are instances where this is the case. Politicians that take bribes to fuel their careers, partners that abuse their significant others for their own gain, bosses that exploit their workers. I don't think I need to illustrate people that are toxically selfish, we are all well aware of these people.

Their counterpart, though, are those that strive to be the best version of themselves. They actively work to have the body they want, the careers they want and the hobbies that excite them. Not only are these people living in their own accord which makes them better to be around, but they actually inspire others to reach their same heights. When someone goes from morbidly obese to healthy and fit, they set the example it can be done. When a high school dropout climbs from a fast-food employee burger flipper to regional manager they show where you start is not where you end. When a heroine addict gets clean, finds love and starts a family it shows no matter how bad things get there's still hope.

By focusing on yourself you truly make the biggest impact that you can. Imagine what the world would be if everyone strived to reach their highest potential. Rather than having your attention on the problems of the world, center back on what you need to do.

Age

Another anecdote I wanted to share on the concept of feeling ready ties to our age. Another cliché I love is, "age is just a number." It's true though. There are those who are young at heart, that push the envelope, and explore their curiosity throughout their entire lives. There are those who have also resigned their life and given up very early in their youth. You are never too old or too young to start something new. I have to say especially for older folks, I find it so inspiring to see more elderly people trying something new. If you're in your sixties and it's your first time on a snowboard that's awesome. If you're in your sixties and you decide now is the time to quit smoking to enjoy the rest of your life with your kids hats off to you. You want to be a musician in your thirties and you've never held a note in your life, props on your courage. It's easy to think it's too late to start something. Those who are successful did it when they were younger. Stop comparing yourself to them though. Yes, it takes time to start something new, but the time will pass regardless. Start it now so you're not wishing you started it earlier.

Nothing to Lose, Everything to Gain

Lastly, I would like to end this chapter with another thought pattern I practice that I call nothing to lose, everything to gain. Especially when I'm at a crossroads of choosing between two options this serves me well. I imagine all the outcomes of a situation, really imagine what could happen and then become content with all of the potential scenarios.

Take going out on a date. Say it's off an app so you really aren't quite sure who this person will be or what to expect. For me I'd say there are a few ways it could go. One we have no chemistry and meetup, don't really vibe, and go home. I tried, I'm no better or worse for the experience. Second option, they're truly awful. They're rude to me or the people we are around, they're loud and obnoxious, I have a terrible time, but now I have a hilarious story for this awful date I went on. Third they're absolutely charming, we have a tremendous time and it leads to fruitful experience. Now, we all likely would prefer the third experience, but hopefully you've begun to adopt the attitude that we can only control our own behavior, our own experience.

Everything else is in the hands of other people, the universe, fate, whatever you want to call it, but basically outside forces. When you are content with any outcome you are free.

Another example from my life was the opportunity to live and work in Japan or stay in Denver. In Denver, I had grown a wonderful group of friends, had great living arrangement, an ok job, but had recently become a yoga instructor and was keen to grow that part of my life. I also had the option to work in a hostel in Japan for three months. Those experiences are so drastically different I think it's impossible to really compare. Ultimately, I decided Japan, but in my head had I stayed that would have been equally rewarding in a different way.

That's how many of the choices you make will go. Traveling for years or working on a career. They're fulfilling in very different ways. At some point you do have to choose too. Know there's no wrong answers though. There's no mistakes.

You take a job you end up hating. Great. Doing tasks you hate provides you with a lot of valuable information. It keeps you from doing them again. Little by little you will begin to piece together the puzzle of your life and the picture will get clearer and clearer.

My last little bit of optimism for you too is that the "worst" moments or the times when everything goes according to the plan are the least interesting stories of all. How was your camping trip, "oh we drove there, it was nice, perfect weather and got back just in time for work."

Or, "the car broke down and then we hitchhiked with this crazy ex-con in the back of a pickup, are cellphones died right before a tornado hit and there was a shootout in our motel parking lot." Maybe that's a bit exaggerated and would actually be horrifying to experience, but I'd listen to that story over the former.

Undoubtedly the longest and broadest ranging chapter of this book, this section will entail building a mental arsenal of tools for you to use. I say tools because often we are given broad ideas or concepts as a one-size-fits all solution. "Never give up, ..." While these are often great ideas and can work well when applied, there are times when you need to discriminate when to use them. That is why I suggest these ideas for you are like a toolbox.

A hammer and a wrench serve very different functions. A blender and a spatula. A guitar and a pickaxe. All of these are useful, but for different reasons and to different ends. As ridiculous as some of those comparisons may be, there are times when advice, words of wisdom, parables do not apply.

For example, the idea, "Never Give Up!" No matter what obstacles you face, no matter how hard the journey is, always persevere! Sounds great when a motivational speaker is hyping you up. May not be the best words to cling to if you're summiting a peak, in the middle of a blizzard, no visibility, temperatures dropping. That might be a good situation to pack your bags and attempt the summit another time. You've dated someone on again and off again. They cheat, you fight, it always ends in tears... might it is time to "give up" on that relationship and try again with someone new.

With almost if not every single piece of insight I share with you there will be exceptions to the rule, times when they don't apply and scenarios in which to ignore what I say. That's one hundred percent ok. The frustrating question you may have then is, "how do I know when to follow what you say and when to ignore it?" Unsatisfyingly and honestly, I will tell you it depends.

You will find that through your own experiences, your own trials and errors you will find what works for you. Your intuition will grow and you will become more confident in your decision making ability. I really challenge you to take the ideas I'm presenting you and think them over. Really play with them and think how they may or may not serve you. A simple changing of perspective can often be just as helpful as changing behaviors.

Chapter 17

Comparison

We live in a social hierarchy. There is no question about that. Poor, middle class, one-percenters. We have many ways of organizing ourselves. We have supervisors, managers, directors and presidents. The advent of social media has only exacerbated our ability to rank ourselves.

How many likes we get or followers we have, there are limitless ways to judge and sort ourselves. This constant need to see how we fit in with the world mostly works to our detriment.

It keeps us down, makes us feel inferior, and stops us from progressing. On your journey of improvement keeping score of everyone else will only serve as a distraction. There is only one person you should you be in competition with and measure yourself up to.

That person is yourself.

There are always going to be people ahead of you. No matter what endeavor or benchmark you want to set, someone will always be ahead. Maybe they started younger than you, maybe they're genetically predisposed to be stronger, maybe nepotism allowed them more opportunities. There is an infinite number of reasons others will be ahead of you and you will never catch up.

It doesn't matter. You don't need to be better than they are. What you need to be is the best version of yourself. The more you hone your craft, the more you practice, the better you will become.

Your competition is between you and your past self. When you look at yourself remember where you started. Change is gradual. It takes time, persistent effort and patience to notice differences. One day all the efforts add up. Little by little all your work will make you into the person you aspire to be.

Let go of everyone else. They are on their journey's; their progress is no concern of yours. We are all on our own unique path. We may share similar destinations, but the road we take to get there will never be the same. Rather than being bitter that someone has your dream job and your stuck in the rat race, be inspired. They are proof that you can do it too.

Chapter 18

Removing Poisons

Removing poisons from your life by far will be one of the most challenging undertakings you will go through. We all knowingly or unknowingly have objects in our lives that shackle us to our self-imposed prisons. Poisons exist in many forms. Some are obvious, others are more insidious, sometimes even disguised as allies. Throughout this chapter I will highlight many of the poisons that held me back and my own journey to overcome them. Note that these are highly personal and will very greatly amongst individuals. You will need to take a hard-honest look at your life and your relationship with these entities. Only you will really know what steps are necessary to overcome them.

Technology/Videogames/Internet

This is a broad section. I can't possibly cover every addiction that exists within this sphere, but I believe the lessons I learned can be applied to many arenas. I grew up with a severe videogame addiction. Awkward, shy and socially isolated as a child, videogames were my escape. I felt infinitely more immersed and connected to these worlds and characters than anything I experienced in reality. This obsession led me on a path where I felt destined to one day create my own and work in this field.

Distinctly I remember several occasions where a hobby or passion showed signs of addiction. During my summers I didn't play outside, I gamed. I remember waking up at the crack of dawn and getting on to my Xbox. Hours later a friend joined, we played for a while and he said he was going to get something to eat. I thought that was a good idea. Hours later he returned, noticing I was still on the same game and asked if I ever left. I had not.

If this were a fluke or even every once in a while, likely would not have been an issue. But from my earliest days as a child that I can remember until I was 16 years old, this was my life. School and videogames. Nothing else mattered. At 16 years old, a cataclysmic event shifted my relationship with games, my relationship with material possessions and the crux of my identity.

During a sleep over, I left my game collection outside in my car. The next day I drove home and invited friends over for one of our gaming parties. I went to my car to retrieve my collection and realized I had been robbed in the night.

I couldn't quite process what I was experiencing. Pure rage engulfed me. My friends were there but I couldn't see or hear I was so enthralled by this experience. Up until that point every dollar I ever earned went towards buying games. I prided myself that I earned them. Now in the blink of an eye, unbeknownst to me in my sleep it was stolen. It was as though everything I had ever worked for and who I was vanished in an instant. At the time, I was coping with depression by cutting and without a thought I went to my room and tore open my leg with a knife.

A gash roughly 6 inches long, an inch or so deep, millimeters from my femoral artery brought me back to consciousness. I knew I had to go to the hospital then and was quickly rushed. Friends and family surrounded me horrified. No one knew I coped this way. No one knew I was capable of this. Fortunately, the blade did not reach that artery, which surely would have caused me to bleed out and die within minutes. Afterwards, I distanced myself heavily from games. Years passed and I took a hard-abstinent approach to the medium. Eventually, however, I was able to return and form a healthy relationship with games.

One theme I will illustrate throughout this section is there's no absolute answer. Sometimes things need to be removed entirely from our lives, other times there's space where we can have them and be balanced.

Now I hardly ever play games. The occasional artistic masterpiece from developers I admire will catch my eye and keep me entertained for the duration of its story, and then I'm usually done. Videogames really have the potential to be an incredible medium.

They combine storytelling, art, and music in ways that is breathtaking to behold. The synesthesia of all these devices is remarkable when they are in harmony. For those reasons, I hold space for a game to come along and be part of my life. The next section differs greatly in that for me abstinence was the only way.

Alcohol

Nothing has ever turned my life so upside down the way alcohol did. It captured me and tore through my life like a never-ending hurricane. For 6 years I lived in a state of constant regret, shame and hopelessness. This was one of my hardest journeys, but one I believe will benefit the most.

Just like many Americans, I began drinking in college at the age of 18. I had drunk a few times in high school, even gotten very wasted on a few of occasions, but it really wasn't part of my life in a meaningful way. Freshman year changed everything.

Alcohol flowed easily and brought with it so many tantalizing aspects it was impossible to refuse. Growing up socially awkward and distant I now had this elixir that made me fearless. Suddenly talking to strangers wasn't a chore, it was fun. Not only that, but now there was more opportunity to socialize than ever before.

Have a bottle, have some beer, strangers suddenly want to be your friend. I had a chance to feel popular, to feel important. I did not date much as a teenager and now I was surrounded by beautiful women. It felt too good to be true, and it was.

Maybe not the first night, but by the first week, I was already blacking out. Started harmless enough with some drunk texts, nothing most people haven't done. But that quickly escalated. Soon I was starting fights. I'd make lewd comments, I'd be utterly creepy. I'd steal and leave a wake of destruction behind me.

This cycle then led to me waking up, hearing what I'd done and feel utterly shamed. I would apologize and say how sorry I felt, but after a while, apologies don't mean anything. I never intended to get as drunk as I did, but it happened regardless. Eventually I isolated which made me more depressed and I drank more.

I tried everything in my power to bring alcohol under control. I took month breaks to reset my tolerance. I'd have a glass of water in between drinks or a meal beforehand to slow down how fast it digested. At one point I bought a keychain breathalyzer which lasted all of one night. For 6 years this is how I lived.

I'd be forced out of one group, find a new community and then after drinking be forced to move on again.

For the longest time, I saw no alternatives. The idea of not drinking didn't seem like an option. How would I have friends, how would I date, how would I ever have fun? I knew I was an alcoholic, but these questions made me feel like it was an intrinsic part of life.

Ironically, while I was living in Australia, I finally broke the cycle. Australia is famous or infamous for its' drinking culture. I was convinced that I would find community or connection amongst such a fun-loving culture. That was not my fate though. You can't run from your problems and they followed me all the way down under.

The same patterns of fighting and social isolation persisted. One night, I got into a bar fight and had to be hospitalized for a massive gash across my forehead. I can't tell you what I said or did, but when a stranger breaks a bottle on your head, it can't be good. That didn't get me to stop drinking. Coming to the next day, I remember thinking, "maybe I should lay off, take it easy for a bit." The very next night, I was already back at it.

No there wasn't one ah-ha moment that got me to quit. No cataclysmic fight or bad night to realize enough was enough. Life had been a series of never-ending rock bottoms. Believe me when I say to there is no rock-bottom. Life can always sink lower. Finally, the exhaustion of my existence made me reflect and accept my reality. I was sitting in my dorm room defeated and I finally accepted my life for what it was. I didn't know how to live without alcohol, but I knew there would be no future if I continued.

I stopped, then and there, never looked back. I was lucky that I didn't have cravings like so many recovering alcoholics do. There was a finality for me that knew there was nothing to go back to, but it was a hard road.

I looked to forums for people in recovering. I sought inspiration on YouTube for people who had overcome and how they did it. I slowly and painfully learned how to navigate social situations. I learned how to be comfortable saying no to alcohol and how to respond when people asked why I don't drink. A whole book could be written on just that journey, but more so the intent of this section is to illustrate that it was a choice I had to make of complete abstinence.

There is no option for me to go back and have a couple drinks. There's no moderation or balance for me when it comes to alcohol. I say this to highlight that if this is an arena you are thinking about you need to be really honest.

Some people party hard in their twenties, cut back and find a glass of wine or two serves them. Alcohol can bring a lot of fun and joy. As much as it destroyed me, there are nights that were still great, memories I'm fond of, and because of how things worked out I don't regret any of it. All of it was necessary.

You will have to decide for yourself what your relationship to alcohol, or other drugs may be. The final thing I will leave you on this subject is this. If you think you have a problem or might have one, you probably do. People that have a healthy relationship with alcohol don't think about that.

People

People can be just as cancerous to your health as any foreign substance. In some ways this is one of the hardest things to tackle. It's easy to understand quitting cigarettes, booze, or fast food; it's quite another thing to cutout friends or family.

Ever heard of the expression misery loves company? Well that's the essence of toxic people. They come in many forms and varieties. Some people are constant complainers. Their job sucks, life's not fair, their partner is a disappointment, a seemingly never-ending barrage of negativity. We all need to vent our frustrations, but for some it's more than that. They don't work on themselves or their problems, instead you are their vessel. Know these are not some benign interactions, their energy will bring you down. Unless you are absolutely trapped as coworkers or some other relationship, do your best to remove these people from your life.

Family can be very difficult in this regard. Some family members will do everything they can to shape you to who they want you to be. They'll tell you what career you should have, when you should get married, when to have kids. Sometimes it's advice from a loving place, other times it's them trying to justify how they lived.

If they got married young and had kids right away, you should too. If they gave up time at home for their career you should too. If they quit their dreams to work a steady job so should you.

Where I was raised these were the cultural norms. Many of my family is filled with these types. Full of plenty of alcoholics too. People I wouldn't give a second of time to if we weren't related and at one point, I stopped making that justification.

I have no space, no time or patience for these toxic types. I don't hold a grudge though and I would urge you to do the same. I have an uncle that suffered from debilitating alcoholism. For years I would see him and he would be this empty husk. Lifeless and dead inside, operating solely on alcohol. Throughout that time, I wanted nothing to do with him. Now he's clean and sober and I would be happy to share space with him.

I went through my own time of being an absolute piece of shit. We all make mistakes. We all learn and grow. We need to have space for forgiveness and compassion. We also need to respect ourselves and set boundaries.

When you cut someone out or stop talking it makes them reconsider their behavior. If you don't, what reason do they have to change? These are not easy choices to make. It's hard to know when someone is being an ass for a little while, maybe they are going through a rough patch. Other times it's who they are and they need to change. For your own sanctity and salvation, creating boundaries and removing toxic people is an absolute essential.

Conclusion

Reaching this section, I realize that another book could be written on this subject. As far as addictions go I've battled countless. From coffee, to porn, weed, fast food, even and self-help obsession which itself can become a toxic poison. I wrestled with these and many more. Some things I've found a balance, others I've removed entirely. Your journey may overlap mine; it may be entirely different. I hope that by presenting you with these ideas you can make your own choices and live an intentional life that brings you into harmony.

Chapter 19

Procrastination

Possibly the biggest culprit behind our lack of progress is procrastination. We can all name tasks we *should* be doing but aren't. Tasks we're putting off, we'll get to later, just don't have the time for right now. Procrastination takes on many forms, but the effect is all the same. This force is a relentless enemy you will have to combat and here I will offer you some guidance on how exactly to go about it.

First is putting things off. This is an absolute pillar of procrastination. The more you delay, the longer you wait, the worse it becomes. Sometimes quite literally. Like with cleaning dishes where a mess becomes larger with each passing day. Often times, however, this resistance simply becomes more of a mental barrier.

The longer you delay your responsibilities, the more you build it in your head as this large obstacle to overcome. The longer this continues, the worse it becomes. Suddenly a chore that seemed annoying or difficult, becomes this unconquerable monster you are dreading overcoming. Deal with it right away and you avoid this trap.

Dealing with something at the beginning has many advantages. For one thing, you get to end your day on a high note. Let's take ourselves back to being a child, having to do homework. Say you're given the option of playing for a few hours and getting your work done or doing it right now and then having the rest of the day to yourself. Children who are often prone to immediate gratification may choose to play first, but this is not the way. There is a reciprocal relationship between rest and relaxation.

The harder you work, the better it will feel to rest. As such, if a child does their homework first then they can have the rest of the time to enjoy themselves. What a mood killer it is to be having fun and then having to shut it all down to get to work. The other component is that if you chose fun first, your enjoyment will be tainted by distraction.

Staying present and truly enjoying yourself is quite difficult when you know there are responsibilities waiting for you. It's not impossible, but if I'm lying on my couch, trying to immerse myself in a new TV series and in the back of my head I know there's a mountain of dishes waiting for me, some part of me will always be thinking about this.

Say you're just absolutely spent on this day. Yes, there is a pile of dishes, but you had a long day at work, and you're just absolutely not in the mood. Screw it, you'll just deal with it in the morning. You head to bed and call it a night. Again, you may truly be the master of your headspace and dealing with it the next day doesn't bother you. However, most would find that as they are drifting off, you'll be thinking about the task waiting for you. Trying to slip into an exhausted sleep, in the back of your head you'll know that when you wake up in the morning, the dishes have to get done.

In this situation you could have saved yourself a lot of grief and mental freedom by just doing the work. Taking the five or ten minutes to clean the dishes and put them away could have given yourself freedom and enjoyment. Could have watched your show with ease, went to bed with a clear head and woken up without having to concern yourself with an extra chore. It's beyond simplistic but doing the things you **need** to do will allow you the freedom to do the things you **want** to do.

Another insidious form of delay is what I have termed productive procrastination. Something I'm sure we are all familiar with, productive procrastination is a mismanagement of your priorities. In college I would find my dorm room became a lot cleaner when there was a paper I didn't want to write. Suddenly I would decide now is a good time to do laundry. Cleaning your room, doing laundry, those are positive things, why is that procrastination? Are those not productive ways of spending your time, was there not an entire chapter dedicated towards tidying your space? Yes to both, however there is a proper time and place for everything.

Often the tasks we need to accomplish most are the ones we are least interested in. There is something truly almost magic about this connection and you will find that it can often serve as a great guide to you. When you find a task that you **KNOW** you should be doing, but would rather do anything else, I implore you to challenge yourself and tackle it head on.

Growing up with intense social anxiety, shyness, awkwardness, dating for me was very challenging and although I wanted to connect with women, I was paralyzed by fear. I would go online, read blogs, read books, watch channels on YouTube. I consumed so much material on socializing I became an intellectual expert on all the theories and ideas behind social interactions.

I would spend my money on improving my wardrobe, I got a trendy haircut, spent months and years at the gym improving my physique, on and on doing everything I could to become a more desirable person. You know the thing I did least? Actually, talking to women.

Why? A million reasons. Fear of rejection, lack of self-esteem, thinking any interaction would go poorly so why bother, thinking my body or clothes wasn't good enough, thinking I didn't have enough friends, enough money, thinking I wasn't enough period.

One common theme of procrastination amongst people is age. Too old to start learning guitar, wish I did it when I was younger. Too young to try out standup comedy, who would listen to someone as young as me. Too overweight to go to the gym, didn't go to a prestigious enough school to apply for that position. So many limiting beliefs stop people from even getting started and it is such a tragedy.

To quote a Chinese proverb. *"The best time to plant a tree was 20 years ago, the second-best time is now."* Yes, it would have been great to learn that second language when you were a kid. Would have made things a lot easier. Would have been great to keep up piano when you had all that free time. Think how good you would be now. Would have been great to lose that weight in your twenties. Would have been great to have finished your degree back when you had less responsibilities. But you didn't and now you're here. All those regrets, woulda coulda shouldas, don't serve you in any way at all.

It is too late to go back and do all the things you "should" have done. Times gone, it's over, nothing can be done about that. Rather than cry over the past, do what you need to do now. All the things you wish you did when you were younger do them now. Think of it like giving your future self a gift. What a gift it will be in the future and you will not believe how grateful you will be to have done it.

Prior to getting sober, I knew the challenges that were ahead of me. I was in my early twenties where all of the socializing I had done almost all revolved around drinking. Essentially all dating I had done involved getting drinks, going to a bar, meeting at a party, etc. Socializing which I had never been good at, "learned" if you could call it that, all came from drinking. I knew I would be starting from square one. I look back on it and know now that much of my hesitation came from it.

Eventually I had to grind through it. I went to parties and weddings where there was drinking in copious amounts. Dealt with the peer pressure to drink. Dealt with the onslaught of questions of "why aren't you drinking?" "you're never gonna drink again, ever?" "what made you stop." Feeling like an outsider, feeling like there was something wrong with me, I was the weird one. As with any hard task though it became easier over time. Eventually it just became part of my identity. To this day there are some people that still give me odd looks, still give me shit, don't respect my decision and I just know that we won't connect. That's ok. You don't have to connect with everyone.

Now it is truly easy. I don't think about how I will have to act or what I will say to people, it's just who I am. Take it or leave it.

When you face the challenges you are putting off, you will likely incur similar challenges. People may not respect what you're doing, may put you down as a beginner, but if you keep with it you will overcome their doubts.

If you pick up a guitar and start strumming it may be awhile before you produce something pleasant on the ears. People may laugh, tell you to quit, but their voices exist to comfort their own egos. They are likely so afraid to try something and fail that they have to put you down to comfort their own identity. They would never have the courage to attempt what you are trying.

This can be a great instance to turn their negativity into fuel for your own fire. I'm not the biggest advocate of this mentality. I really think you should pursue dreams because it resonates with you, but I will say there can be a power in doing something to prove someone else wrong. Many famous actors, musicians, inventors and other creators have described how they were surrounded by nay-sayers and they kept at it to one day be able to prove them wrong. If that serves you, I don't think there's anything inherently wrong with it. I do feel you are still operating under some pretense of caring about their opinions, but if that fire fuels your engines in the right directions go for it.

Don't be afraid to suck at something. You will find one of the most rewarding things in life is getting better at something. Whether that's guitar, rock climbing, writing, dancing whatever. As you go through your journey and see how far you've come you will look back with immense satisfaction. It is sincerely one instance where being a beginner is advantageous, you notice the improvements a lot quicker.

*Challenge: Ask yourself and be ruthlessly honest about what you are procrastinating. What task do you **NEED** to do? What scares you, what have you been putting off for the right time or a more convenient date? When you know what this task is make one effort towards getting it done* ***TODAY***.

Chapter 20

Meditation

Of all the practices I have incorporated that have allowed me control over my life, nothing is more beneficial than meditation. If you were take one lesson from this book I would hope it would be learning this practice. Meditation is not just for the yogis and the spiritually inclined. It has been used throughout history across many cultures. From Socrates to Napoleon, Steve Jobs to Siddhartha, these icons of our past understood the importance of meditation.

For years I have practiced meditation daily. Doing so I have experience profound changes in my life. Meditation flows over into every aspect of your life. How glasses allow those with vision impairments to see clearer with their eyes, meditation allows us to see clearer with our minds.

Especially in this modern age, meditation is more important than ever. Our minds are bombarded with constant stimuli. From our screens inundating us with advertisements, the news, social-media, as well as an endless stream of entertainment. This doesn't even scratch the surface of our own lives. Managing our friendships, families, career goals, relationship goals... Our lives and our minds are filled to the brim.

With so many outside influences pulling at our attention is it any wonder we struggle to break free of our old ways? That we fail to start and maintain new healthy habits? With all these factors it's not surprising, but this is the world we live in and if you want to be successful you have to navigate it. Meditation will be one of your greatest allies.

It will allow you to see clearer, be more present, delineate tasks and allow you to drive your own destiny. Beyond these there are a myriad of scientific studies and journals that have shown meditation helps to alleviate depression, anxiety, stress, and other mental illnesses. It has been shown to increase memory retention and learning ability. Entire books have been written on the benefits of meditation and my intent here is simply to give you the tools you need to take control of your life.

Adopt meditation and you will be well on your way to seizing your destiny. There are many schools, many different practices, many different ideas on what meditation is. I encourage to experiment to find the one that resonated with you.

I will leave you with a series of resources and recommendations on where you may find a more thorough explanation of different meditation practices. Hopefully this will lead you to find a practice that suits you. I will also describe my personal practice, provide links and interactive guides available on my website.

My Practice

For my practice I have a delineated place in my bedroom that I use solely for meditation. I have a blanket I sit on, as well as a pillow for my lower back to offer support. This space is only for meditation and I am the only one allowed to use it. Having a sacred space is not necessary, but I believe it is beneficial. I prefer keeping the room as dark as possible, but if you prefer the light that works too. Many practice outside which can be wonderful. I prefer limiting the amount of potential distractions, but this is where you will have to find a method that suits your needs.

I sit cross-legged, eyes closed and back straight against the wall. Some people prefer lying down, others in a chair, some meditate while standing or walking. For me sitting upright specifically brings me to the mental space of knowing I am using this time to meditate and that serves me best.

After finding a comfortable seated position, I begin focusing on my breath. In and out. Every exhale I count and go from ten to one. I do this until I am entirely focused on my breath. Often during the counting my mind will wander to the day ahead, things that need to be done, what I will do next. When I notice my mind has wandered, I simply return my attention to counting. You will undoubtably find as you meditate your mind wanders. This is entirely okay and to be expected. No need to punish yourself or get frustrated. Simply notice your mind has drifted and bring it back.

As a novice meditator and as even an experienced meditator you will find your mind loves to wander. It is quite comical in fact how difficult a simple task like focusing on your breath for ten counts can be. Suddenly thoughts of what you were doing earlier, or a conversation you will have in the future, what sounds good for dinner, come creeping in out of nowhere. As I was taught, do not get mad or disappointed that you lost focus. It's completely normal and natural.

The "ah-hah" moment of meditation for me is realizing I got distracted. My mind came back on, I lost count and forgot about my breath. No need to punish yourself or be upset, simply realize what happened and bring your attention back to your breath.

Once I feel like I am truly absorbed on my breath I stop counting. I retain my awareness of breath, but then I begin a body scan or what is often described in yoga as a rotation of consciousness. Many yogis have orthodox rules on how this is to be conducted, often from the right hand, the toes or inside the mouth. There are reasons behind this that are valid, but I prefer starting from the crown of the head.

I notice the crown of my head. I see how it feels. Is there any tension? Are there any areas I'm tense or holding stress in? Then I descend to my forehead, eyebrows, jaw, neck, shoulders, etc. The entire body. After that I bring awareness to how I'm feeling. I notice how my thoughts have slowed. I aim to reach a point of utter stillness where no thoughts arise and I am simply present.

Personally, I feel the most beneficial meditations exist in the 20 to 40-minute range. I have found outside of this range I don't notice much of a difference. There's also only so much time in a day. 20 to 40 minutes seems like a fair amount of time, without being too much to commit to in the modern world.

I would **strongly** urge building up to this though. Starting out at 5 minutes can be surprisingly challenging. Unless you were raised with a practice or were taught benefits of moments of reprieve, most people now are constantly plugged in and engaged. Whether that's to their phone, the tv, friends, music, work, whatever your distraction is, most people do not have moments of silence to just sit for them.

If you are a total novice to meditation, I would suggest starting at 5 minutes. Set a timer on your phone or another device to go off so you don't have to worry about it and just focus on breath. Once you are comfortable and can do this maybe add 30 seconds, maybe a minute. Ease into it and don't feel like you need to be in double digits right away. Even if you sat just for one minute taking that time for yourself will truly be impactful.

Rotation Of Consciousness

Here I will outline a more detailed version of the body scan I mentioned earlier. After you have brought attention to your breath, the next step to dive deeper into your awareness is performing a rotation of consciousness. Notice whether or not you are holding any tension and release. The process should be relatively quick, no need to dwell or hold your focus for extended periods of time. Simply notice the sensations you feel. Different yoga and meditation practitioners will have variations on this. Some will incorporate more body parts, others fewer. Experiment and find what method works best for you.

Starting from the top, bring your attention to the crown of your head. Now your forehead. Your right eyebrow, your right eye. Your left eyebrow, your left eye. The space between your eyebrows. Bring your attention to your nose. Your upper lip, your lower lip. Your left cheek, your right cheek. Your jaw. Bring your attention to your left ear and your right.

The left side of your neck. The right side of your neck. The back of your neck

Bring your attention to your right collarbone. The back of your right shoulder. The front of your right shoulder. Your bicep, your triceps, the elbow, the back of your forearm, the front of your forearm and your wrist. Focus on your pinky, ring finger, middle finger, pointer finger, thumb, the back of your hand and the front of your hand.

Bring your attention to your left collarbone. The back of your left shoulder. The front of your left shoulder. Your bicep, your triceps, the elbow, the back of your forearm, the front of your forearm and your wrist. Focus on your pinky, ring finger, middle finger, pointer finger, thumb, the back of your hand and the front of your hand.

Focus on your right side of your chest, the left side of your chest. The center of your chest. Your left abdomen, your right abdomen, your navel and your groin.

Focus on your right shoulder blade, your left shoulder blade. The back of your right ribs, the back of your left ribs. Your lower right back, your lower left back. The spine and your tail bone.

Focus on your right buttocks. The hamstring, the quad, knee, shin and calf. Notice the heel of your foot, ball of the foot and the top of the foot. Your little toe, second toe, third toe, fourth toe and big toe.

Focus on your left buttocks. The hamstring, the quad, knee, shin and calf. Notice the heel of your foot, ball of the foot and the top of the foot. Your little toe, second toe, third toe, fourth toe and big toe.

Finally notice your entire body. Notice how your mind feels. Are you calmer, more relaxed? This is my preferred method. I highly encourage you to preform this method or some variation. Experiment and find a method that works for your needs.

Challenge: Sit for five minutes. Find a comfortable place to sit, either on a cushion on the floor or in a chair, wherever is easiest for you to sit still. Then pull out your phone, set a timer for 5 min and sit. Eyes closed or open, take 5 minutes for yourself. Afterwards take notice of how you felt. Was it difficult or easy? Did your mind race? Do you feel calmer?

If you are interested in guided meditations I have several available on my website www.willowenblack.com and through my social-media platforms @the.balanced.self

Chapter 21

Balance

Another immensely therapeutic and grounding practice that I could not overstate the benefits of is journaling. Journaling is like a swiss army knife in terms of uses. There are numerous ways it can benefit you. Here I will outline many of the ways it has impacted me and suggestions on how you might build your own practice.

Journaling to me is one of the greatest forms of catharsis. My mind has a tendency to race and to become obsessed with thoughts. All day I'll be going in circles dwelling on ideas I can't shake. By putting my thoughts to paper I'm able to clear my head of this chatter.

For the visual learners, I believe it also allows us to see our issues from a new perspective. Writing your thoughts down, seeing them for what they are, allows us some much-needed space to not be overwhelmed. I discussed earlier the notion of worry. When I write out my greatest concerns, I start seeing that they really aren't as bad as I've made them out to be. They become much more manageable.

Another beneficial aspect of journaling is it allows us to track our progress. We get to see our journey. Our highs and our lows. For me, journaling is a daily practice. Sometimes it's as simple as writing down what I did, maybe a paragraph or two. Other times I'm going on multiple pages working through different thoughts or issues in my life.

At the end of each month, I write and reflect on how I felt things went. I look at my white board of goals. I asses where I succeeded and where I could improve. Did I hit work out goals? Did I write as much as I wanted? Did I make enough progress on my business? Were there extenuating circumstances that may gotten in my way? I go over all the details and then set intentions for the next month ahead. Where I can improve, tasks I want to focus on, areas I want to make a priority.

I also keep a list of major accomplishments throughout the year on my desktop. Books read, outdoor adventures, travel, business accomplishments, etc. Similar to my monthly goals, at the beginning and end of year I reflect. I take inventory of everything I accomplished, reflect and then make note of what I want to accomplish for the next year.

I've already expressed my disdain for New Year's Resolutions, however, I think there's much value in setting goals for the year to come. I leave room flexibility. You never know what random events might shape your year ahead. Having intentions, having goals will lead you on a path where your life is of your design, and not that of random circumstance.

"If you don't build your own dream someone else will hire you to help build theirs."
– Tony Gaskins Jr.

Gratitude

Another practice deeply tied to this practice is writing a gratitude journal. Gratitude is one of the highest forms of energy we can express. In fact, according to most spiritual teachings it is the peak. Whether or not you have any spiritual inclinations, a gratitude journal is an immensely powerful practice.

Expressing gratitude has numerous benefits. When life showers you with blessings, it's great to acknowledge and be thankful for all your gifts. A long friendship, a new lover, a promotion at work, your pet, these could all be gifts that you may be fortunate enough to have in your life. When life is really in a groove, it's important to reflect and acknowledge these moments. What may be even more powerful, though, is when you are in a rut. When things are at their worst and finding the ability to still practice gratitude.

This in no way is an easy endeavor. When you feel you are at absolute rock bottom, someone telling you to be grateful is likely the last thing you want to hear. I challenge you to really sit with your circumstances and find just one thing to be grateful for.

If you are in the West, you might be suffering from terrible circumstances. Maybe you just had your heart broken, maybe you were fired or let go, maybe someone crashed into your bumper and drove off. You might be dealing with mental illness, addiction or any number of debilitating conditions. Those are all real problems not to be dismissed or put down. But most likely you have a roof over your head. You likely have access to clean water, electricity, you're likely not starving and I'd wager you have access to a stable internet connection.

These might seem like basic necessities and from a humanitarian standpoint and they should be. This is not the reality for much of the world. There are many that go to bed hungry, there are millions that have nowhere to call home. The fact that others have it worse than you does not negate your own problems, but hopefully by contemplating this you might find that you have some good things going for you. This will keep you grounded.

When it comes to keeping a gratitude journal there are an infinite number of ways you could approach it. Some have a designated diary or journal specifically for it. Personally, after my daily entry in my journal I like to write a few sentences saying what I'm grateful for. You can write ten things a day, three things once a week, one entry a week. Find a system that works for you. I would challenge you to make it a consistent practice.

Chapter 22

Balance

Finally, I will leave you with one final piece of insight. With a book like this there's so much to take in. So many concepts and ideas to play with, it can be hard to keep it all straight. Not to overburden you with another one, but rather one idea that will hopefully tie everything together. That concept is balance.

Simple, yet difficult, minimal, but complicated. Finding balance in life to me is the ultimate aim. If I were to summarize my entire ethos to one word it would be balance. The more we grow, the older we get, the more we take on, the harder this can be.

Friends, hobbies, career, time in nature, time with family, our bodies, our minds, the list could be endless. These are all aspects of our life we have to juggle. Life seems to have a funny way of throwing a wrench in our routines the second we get a hang of things too.

There are times you need to work more, times you need to work less. Sometimes you will need connection, others solitude. You will find periods of cultivating your highest self and others where you need to indulge in your shadow.

Part of us wishes we had a roadmap. Some sort of system to know when to do the things we need to. I'm sure other books will convince you there is. I'm here to tell you, life is about learning. Life is figuring out how to spend our days.

We learn what fulfills us, what gives us purpose and meaning. Every day we get a little better at managing our time. Part of the joy of life is going through this process. It would be like skipping to the end of a movie if we had all the answers right away. The journey is where the interesting parts are.

One chapter ends, another begins. We solve one problem, only for another to pop its' head out of the shadows. We explore to discover, to grow and learn. We return home, to rest, reflect and be comforted. A never-ending cycle. Remembering the past, looking forward to the future and finding ourselves here in the present.

That's dualities, that's balance.

www.ingramcontent.com/pod-product-compliance
Lightning Source LLC
Chambersburg PA
CBHW070042120526
44589CB00035B/2267